Back to Earth

Back to Earth

Tomorrow's Environmentalism

ANTHONY WESTON

Temple University Press
Philadelphia

Temple University Press, Philadelphia 19122
Copyright © 1994 by Temple University
All rights reserved
Published 1994
Printed in the United States of America

Library of Congress Cataloging-in-Publication Data

Weston, Anthony, 1954–
    Back to earth : tomorrow's environmentalism / Anthony Weston.
      p. cm.
    Includes bibliographical references (p.) and index.
    ISBN 1-56639-236-5 (cloth : acid-free paper). —ISBN 1-56639-237-3 (pbk. :
acid-free paper)
    1. Environmentalism. 2. Environmental policy. I. Title.
GE 195.W47   1994
363.7—dc20   011008   94-3856

ISBN 13: 978-1-56639-237-2 (pbk. : alk. paper)

021012P

Relation is reciprocity. . . .
Our students teach us, our works form us. . . .
How we are educated by children, by animals!
Inscrutably involved,
we live in the currents
of universal reciprocity.

—Martin Buber
I and Thou

Contents

Acknowledgments

Good friends and colleagues took time to read and discuss this work with me: Tom Birch, Ed Casey, Jim Cheney, Patti Cruickshank-Schott, Amy Halberstadt, Steve Jurovics, Bob Kirkman, Irene Klaver, Tom Regan, John Sullivan. I am indebted to David Abram for the wonderful category "more-than-human." I am grateful to Jane Cullen for unflagging editorial support. I am also grateful for certain more-than-human sources of inspiration, to the owls who still sing in my neighborhood, to the winds and wildflowers of the Wisconsin prairie and certain peaks of the West. The intemperance and obscurity that remain in this work reflect my own impatience and inadequacy. What this work nonetheless offers, I hope, are certain invitations and intimations. Occasional glimpses of something unexpected in some unsuspected clearings in the woods. Some ways to get there. Perhaps even—the possibility of love.

Back to Earth

1

Has Environmentalism Forgotten the Earth?

We live, we are told, in "the decade of the environment." Recycling is up, rainforest beef is out, and every bookstore in America is eager to offer us advice about how to Save the Earth. The 1992 United Nations Conference on the Environment was apparently the largest gathering of world leaders ever, and in the fall of that year the United States even elected an environmentalist vice-president.

And yet . . . and yet. Many environmentalists themselves feel a certain reservation about these very successes—notwithstanding that twenty years ago these were the very things we were calling for. We have lived in other "decades" too, and have gone on to other things. The 1970s were labeled "The Decade of the Environment" by none other than Richard Nixon. Our ecological problems have changed but have not become easier; quite the contrary. Our rivers are less flammable but more persistently afflicted by minute toxins like dioxin. Roadside litter is down, global temperatures are up.

We are all environmentalists now. Yet we stand at no less a distance from the more-than-human world: from "nature," from other animals and natural places. We are no more inclined to acknowledge—certainly not really to *feel*—that we ourselves are at stake with "nature," with the rest of the world: entwined, enveloped, submerged in it. Vanishing species, to take just one example, are only regretted in the way that we might regret the loss of a television series. This is often the same thing; we regret the loss of more interesting episodes on the Discovery Channel, there being no other way that we know or are ever likely to have known anything wild. Meanwhile, by making such a point of the Earth's dependence on us—of the necessity for us to act to "Save the Earth"—we accentuate that very dependency. "The Earth" becomes more like an object of pity, allowing us to hold stronger feelings and personal vulnerabilities at a distance, at bay.

Listen—actually *listen*—to the standard rhetoric about "Saving the Earth," the kind of talk that now surrounds us on all sides.

> No part of the world is free from our dangerous influence. The rainforests of Brazil and the Arctic ice all bear the scars of pollution, or of exploitation. . . . We must now care for all of the living world. Wilderness is a collection of fragile species that must be rescued, nourished, and protected. . . . Our growing interest in nourishing and caring for plants and pets in our private spaces is reflected in the growing knowledge that we must preserve and care for the life of the entire planet.[1]

We are adrift in this kind of rhetoric. But there reasons to be uneasy. For one thing, the image of nature that emerges is that of a virtually helpless ward. The planet is explicitly compared to a *pet;* thus imagined to be utterly dependent, unequal, "fragile," something whose capacities and needs *we* understand, though in fact even our own prior record with respect to our pets is not encouraging. Wilderness is explicitly labeled a *collection* of species, like a kind of unorganized open-air museum: not a living system with its own integrity and with its own dynamics, many of them unknown to us, and perhaps unknowable. Then we are told that "we" must care for "it." Again we move ourselves outside the system entirely. We have been "dangerous"; now we must "care." We are still the chief actors in this play, only now we must take a bit more care for the scenery.

Not to be misunderstood: I do not mean that the world is not in a sense fragile. I do not mean that we can be careless with it. But what is missing is the sense that we are *part* of this system—that it is not somehow "ours," that it has a coherence of its own, depths of order and possibility that we may not even suspect. Most of the action has nothing to do with us. There are interchanges in which humans do not set the terms from the beginning. Nature conserves us, as the Naskapi Indians say, not we it.

Albert Gore, in his remarkable best seller, *Earth in the Balance,* does insist that "we are part of the Earth." If we dump massive amounts of toxic chemicals into the environment, he writes, we should not be surprised when they show up, probably more toxic, somewhere else. We should not be surprised when the climate starts to change and the oceans start to rise. *Earth in the Balance* goes on to propose policies that will ameliorate at least some of this destruction: new fuels, massive conservation initiatives, economic measures that account for ecological costs.

There is more. At points, Gore goes beneath the immediate crisis. A kind of "disconnection," he says, underlies the crisis:

The cleavage in the modern world between mind and body, man and nature, has created a new kind of addiction: I believe that our civilization is, in effect, addicted to the consumption of the Earth itself. This addictive relationship distracts us from the pain of what we have lost: a direct experience of our connection to the vividness, vibrancy, and aliveness of the rest of the natural world. The froth and frenzy of industrialized civilization mask our deep loneliness for that communion with the world that can lift our spirits and fill our senses with the richness and immediacy of life itself.[2]

We have lost the direct experience of the world, says Gore. Hence our "loneliness" and our "addiction." This claim—elaborated, psychologized, historicized at the length of a hundred pages—is extraordinary coming from a contemporary politician. Let us honor Gore for his courage as well as his clarity. He takes an enormous further step, and a risky step for someone in his position, beyond the familiar kind of environmentalism just discussed.

But here too a certain uneasiness arises. Another extraordinary fact: nowhere in that hundred pages does Gore say anything about what that "vividness, vibrancy, and aliveness of the rest of the natural world" or "the richness and immediacy of life itself" *actually come to.* We have indeed lost the direct experience of the world—the "direct experience of real life,"[3] as he puts it elsewhere—but there is almost no direct experience of that world, of that life, in this book. In the end we still see only the fragile, battered, agglomerated, homogenized "environment" featured in the ordinary environmental rhetoric. Gore's book still insistently speaks from a human, urban, economic, and political perspective. Waste-disposal problems, just for one example, are discussed chiefly in terms of economic justice to humans. Costs to other creatures and to ecosystems are seldom and only fleetingly highlighted as harms in their own rights. Obligations to future (human) generations—not the call of other creatures or the future Earth—are invoked in order to justify changes in economic measures to take account of ecological harms.

In short, we still stand at a distance from larger living worlds. Maybe more self-critical, but still at a distance. The invoked possibilities of connection, "vibrancy," and "aliveness" are still hidden behind Gore's critique of incomplete economic measures and his outrage at our "fouling our own nests." He still speaks from the human world rather than from some place in the more-than-human.

Again: not that ecologically sane policies are not desperately needed, not that Gore's approach is not extraordinary even for someone less pressured by public conformity than he. Right now, Earth often *is* "in the balance." The point is that Gore, too, in a more subtle way, stands at a distance from more-than-human worlds. The astonishingly wild possibilities of other animals and natural places still are not even hinted at. The closest we come is, as it were, under the sponsorship of God. When it seems possible for a moment that we might glimpse "an infinite image of God" in them, then Gore allows himself to speak of "the myriad slight strands from the Earth's web of life." Even here, though, nothing specific is said. None of these strands is teased out for wondering eyes to see. Is the world too embarrassing to speak of, even when it turns out, so to speak, to be God's body? Where is the voice of the bowhead whale and the warm wetness of the rains, the stars blazing through the bat-thick, insect-twitching sky?

This is not a new complaint. "Here is this vast, savage, howling mother of ours, Nature, lying all around, with such beauty, and such affection for her children, as the leopard; and yet we are so early weaned from her breast to society, to that culture which is exclusively an interaction of man on man—a sort of breeding in and in."[4] That is Henry David Thoreau, writing in 1862. Philosopher Neil Evernden made a similar complaint a decade ago. Environmentalism, says Evernden, has thoroughly absorbed the prevailing tendency to justify all things by reference to their usefulness to us, and moreover to put these justifications in the most technical, "value-free," and typically abstract language.

> During much of the history of the environmental movement it has been apparent that the incentive to preservation was personal and emotional. . . . But the arrival of ecology and . . . resource management has made it possible to be that contradictory being, a dispassionate environmentalist. . . . This has made the environ-

mental arguments much more presentable to government agencies and to a disinterested public . . . [but] the underlying assumptions have shifted significantly. In learning to use numbers to talk about the world, [the environmentalist] forgets that his initial revolt was partly precipitated by people using numbers to talk about the world.[5]

And again, the problem is not just the use of numbers but the use of an entire abstract vocabulary. Even the term *environment*— and correspondingly the label *environmentalism*—turns out to be a snare. "Environment" literally means "surrounding." The term implicitly refers to something or someone "environed." In this sense it is a relative notion; it supposes a point of reference, something or someone surrounded. And of course that point of reference is—us! "*Our* environment" indeed! Again we present ourselves—just a little more subtly this time—at center stage. Even the idea of "the Earth" in "Save the Earth!" is a massive abstraction. We don't experience "the Earth." What we know, if we're lucky, are the squirrels chasing each other up and down these oak trees, the rumbling of a distant thunderstorm in the dark, the great cycles of the seasons. But "Save the Earth!" is what goes on our bumper stickers. Do we know what we are saying?

We turn to religious imagery. A speech attributed to the Duwamish Indian Chief Seattle ("How can you sell the air . . .?") is widely labeled the "Fifth Gospel." Ecologist Barry Commoner's maxim "Nature knows best" has been called, without a trace of irony, "The Eleventh Commandment." But suppose that the finality and authority of "commandments" is just what the more-than-human does *not* offer? Suppose that here we need to travel light, to walk in, like Thoreau, with just a walking stick and an apple, unsure what we will find, not armed with maps that tell us in advance what we will and should see? Even the "Fifth

Gospel," it turns out, is not what it seems. Though something called "Chief Seattle's speech" has reached the best-seller lists in the form of an illustrated children's book, that version bears at best a distant and often opposite relation to what Seattle apparently actually said. The familiar and much more congenial version was actually written by a Southern Baptist screenwriter in 1971, based—but on some points only very loosely—on a much darker speech attributed, but uncertainly, to the real Seattle.[6]

Professional environmental philosophers try to systematize all environmental values into one unified formula or principle and to discover the "basis" for all such values, to establish them, once and for all, by argument. The conservationist Aldo Leopold is supposed to have given us the formula: "A thing is right when it tends to preserve the integrity, stability, and beauty of the biotic community." But suppose that values *evolve*, like everything else in the more-than-human. Leopold himself, the very patron saint of environmental ethics, in fact insisted on just this evolution, two pages before the formula now cited as final. Values develop, he writes; every summary is tentative. So is his—so is any philosopher's. Remember that even the most fundamental shape of what we take to be "the environmental crisis" has changed with the decades. In the 1960s the problem was pollution: litter on the roads, sewage in the rivers. Now we are worried about global effects, like ozone depletion and global warming. Tomorrow, who knows?

No final answer is possible. Not now, probably not ever, but certainly not now, not with so many new questions and so many new possibilities opening up all at once. We cannot think our way back to the Earth. We can only *work* our way more thoroughly into and around the Earth, from the particular place within it that we already find ourselves: practically, mindfully, open-mindfully. But then what we do *not* need are more commandments or Indian Gospels or calls to arms. We need a different kind of environmentalism.

Here is what this book proposes.

Let us take seriously what Gore says but does not follow up: that we have lost a sense of the "vividness, vibrancy, and aliveness of the rest of the natural world" and "the richness and immediacy of life itself"—that this disconnection, on the deepest level, *is* "the environmental crisis." Let us take seriously the overtones in Seattle's words (or rather, in the scriptwriter's words, appropriating Seattle to speak them—for it is the image of the Indian, however dark his conclusions, that makes those words compelling): that knowing this Earth—always hearing its voices, watching, listening, living without insulation—is a kind of induction into mystery, belonging, rootedness.

Let us take seriously the implicit suggestion that ultimately the answer to "environmental crisis" is some restored sense of that "vibrancy" and that "richness." Recycling, habitat protection, wilderness preservation—of course, yes, this is crucial. But *ultimately* what we require, if we are to understand why we should even care about this Earth, is what Gore calls "direct experience with real life." Let us take seriously Evernden's suggestion that "dispassionate environmentalism," however effective in congressional hearing rooms, ultimately undercuts the very sense of connection to and participation in the more-than-human that environmentalism was supposed to speak for. Let us take seriously the implicit suggestion that we must restore that sense of connection and participation. And restore it *now*—not somehow only as a product of the right policies or principles, as if this too were only a task for the professional philosopher or politician.

This book attempts to reopen that lost sense of possibility: to explore some more-than-human worlds with these concerns in mind. We remember, for one thing, the other animals right next to us: animals that remain with us even now, like cats, dogs, horses, as well as the vast range of other creatures, some quite alien and wild, that have lived and worked with humans historically: pigs, cormorants, bees, weasels, elephants, and many more. Even now, mostly, we live in "mixed communities." Even now, moreover, many social but still wild species, like crows, also live "next" to us.

There are wilder stories, too: children raised by gazelles, whales singing to each other across oceans, the earth singing on the same frequencies as the dreaming brain. Human sociability opens up the possibility not merely of human adoption of other social animals but other animals' "adoptions" of humans, and certainly of deeply shared social worlds. Likewise our senses offer immense, layered, vital worlds to us—again shared and deeply engaging worlds, refracted in a thousand forms all around us. Our music and our speech themselves partly originate in natural sounds and patterns. When we speak of murmuring streams and whispering pines, whippoorwills and chickadees, the winds and the land and the birds themselves speak through us. "The original poetry," writes Gary Snyder, "is the sound of running water and the wind in the trees."[7] He means this literally. The phrase for "it is a fine evening," in the language of the Koyukon Indians, is the phrase the hermit thrushes sing at dusk in their forests. The Earth sings through us.

"Vitality and vibrancy" lie in such details. It is the stories that persuade, and ignite. Behind them, around their edges, we can pose questions about how so profound a rootedness of the human within the nonhuman is possible. The reader need not believe that all of the wilder stories are true. Their truth, in a sense, is not even the main point, though I will suggest that our habit of dismissing the possibilities of the rest of our world is often backed by no experience at all. (Lack of experience, in fact, makes it *possible*.) The real point, the real necessity, is to bring into focus the underlying connections.

Right now we know the *moon* better than the rainforests.[8] Our astronomers are busy sacrificing Mount Graham's endangered

red squirrels for a University of Arizona telescope project. Our space explorers have already pushed the dusky seaside sparrow into extinction by the construction of Cape Canaveral.[9] Yet all of them would be staggered to find the very same creatures on the other end of their telescopes or space probes. *Bacteria* on Mars would have been a tremendous discovery. Imagine finding a mosquito. Imagine finding—a dusky seaside sparrow.

Maybe we can see better from a distance. For a moment, suppose that we imagine Earth an alien planet. Imagine arching down in a long glide or a burst of fire to our very own places, even to our own backyards, finally escaping the merely human claustrophobia of some unimaginable starship with unutterable relief, undertaking our own "Mission to Earth," as some astronauts have actually proposed.[10] Imagine encountering strange beings, enormous or tiny, amorous or ancient perhaps, intricately specialized or preternaturally adaptive, floating, flying, dancing. But then open your eyes: this is our own planet.

> When you listen over a pair of headphones to whales . . . in deep ocean, it's really as though you were listening from within the Horsehead Nebula, or some galactic space that is otherworldly, not part of anything you know, where the boat is floating. Once, on an early fall night, I was coming back from the Arctic, where I had been [studying] bowhead whales in a boat at sea. As we flew down across the Canadian Arctic, we were beneath an arc of northern lights, which were pure green and bell-shaped. We and the plane were the clapper of this bell, with the green light over us. And for the first time in my life I felt that I was in the position of the whale that is singing to you when you're in the boat and just listening to it. That's the kind of space that is somehow illuminated, depicted, made sensible by the hydrophones. It gives you a special impression of the sea. We all love the ocean's beautiful blue sparkle, but beneath it, down deeper, whales are moving with the slow drifting currents, whales that are great, gentle cloudlike beings.[11]

Great, gentle cloudlike beings; genuinely alien and yet co-inhabitants of our own world, once so crowding the seas that they were regularly reported as navigational hazards,[12] hunted worldwide to the brink of extinction for lamp oil and perfume; but still there, even if barely, in some places, at least. The oceans still sing. A cat hunches over this very desk as I write, bats hang under your eaves, one hundred million monarch butterflies migrate, every year, four thousand miles, from the northern United States and Canada to winter on the California coast, following what nature writer John Hay calls "nature's great headings," invisible to us.[13] Even now, with all our blazing cities, bioluminescent currents and eddies in the ocean are the last light departing astronauts see from earth.[14] A species of leaf-eating weevil, one inch long, camoflauges itself by carrying a forest of tiny ferns and mosses in crevasses on its back; still tinier insects live in that forest. Worlds within worlds. Bacteria live in rocks three miles below the surface of the Earth; the latest theory is that life on Earth may have originated in the interior and that subterranean bacteria and other forms of life feeding on the planet's chemical and thermal energy (and equally possible on, or rather *in,* other planets too, by the way) actually outweigh all life on the surface.[15] Our own bodies harbor billions of bacteria, while we ourselves may play a role like our bodies' bacteria in the larger living organism that is now supposed, by some scientists, to include all life on Earth.[16]

We live in a bizarre and wild place. We live in the midst of life so immense, so weirdly varied, so pervasive, that perhaps it is no surprise that we have had to tune some of it out in order to function at all. That humans evolved from apes is still controversial in some quarters, but the newspapers this week have been speaking of the latest theory: that humans and *fungi* share a relatively recent evolutionary ancestor.[17] We can't deal with it. But yet we must; and we must deal with it now, if we are not truly to turn the whole world into the desolate and utterly humanized wasteland that too many of us already inhabit.

So this book has a second aim. To reopen a lost sense of possibility, first; but then to ask how—practically, concretely, *now*—we can live out some of those possibilities. Seeing ourselves once again as "part of this Earth"—another phrase of Gore's that this book aims to give a genuine, concrete, experienced meaning—still may sound very much like something that goes on only in a person's head. But more than attitudes are at stake. Snyder writes of the necessity of what he calls "wild etiquette": the sense that our comportment matters, in fact matters fundamentally, and as much toward larger living worlds and specific other nonhumans as toward other humans. The proposal in this book is that he is right in the most literal sense. My intention is to explore in the most literal sense—even in the most pedestrian sense, as Snyder does not—what this proposal might actually mean. How shall we now live?

There is no single answer. There are only a multiplicity of possibilities, springing up everywhere, like a genuine revolution, like weeds in the garden. Consider "quiet zones," for one example: new settings, deliberately protected areas, where cars, lawnmowers, stereos, and their kin do not define the soundscape, therefore a life shared with the more-than-human in the simplest ways: winds, birds, silence. Consider walking. Consider the actual reconstruction of neighborhoods, houses, bikeways, fields, gardens, and much more. New kinds of houses, new kinds of holidays. Attention to the intersections of human and nonhuman places, where encounters can occur. Attention to (re)constructing the day-to-day conditions of nonhuman as well as human spontaneity.

No doubt new kinds of houses and new kinds of holidays are not quite what one expects. It is easier to bemoan the lost wilderness than to try to teach your children the constellations in your backyard. But even Thoreau at his cabin on Walden Pond, who it gratifies us to think of as a hermit, almost as "standing alone in the wilderness," in fact lived within a mile of Concord and walked there nearly every day to see his family. He lived close enough to the road that he could smell the smoke of passing pipe smokers. Fellow townspeople and farmers fished in the pond; the railroad went by one edge of it. The classic meditation on the human relation to nature, written from virtually within the city limits of Concord? But how appropriate! The "rest of the world" is not somewhere else, but right here. Correspondingly, the way "back" might just be a little different than we think.

With respect to other creatures, meanwhile, even the most elementary politeness requires at least thinking about how other creatures might care to live with *us* (or not), rather than taking it upon ourselves to define and thereby limit them too, like the ape language experiments that continued to try to make captive apes use symbolic language, even after ten years or so of research aimed at getting them to *talk* dead-ended when it finally dawned on someone that they don't have our kind of vocal equipment. And once again the essential point is that we have almost no way of knowing, in our present condition, what is truly possible. It is not just that the symbol-using research is a little ambiguous. It is better to ask: on what terms would an ape, say, care to "communicate" with us at all? What could be the "terms" of a dolphin, handless and utterly at home in the waters, who in all probability can "see" inside his or her companions by echolocation[18]—what would language even mean for such a creature?

Better to explore. Jim Nollman plays jazz rhythms with orca and suggests hang-gliding with seagulls: working in their media, as it were, not primarily ours, and going to them in a way that allows them to break off the encounter whenever they wish. Talk about elementary politeness. This is the most basic considerateness of all: not forcing your presence or your projects on another.

Millions of official research dollars pour into "objective" academic research on captive animals—or dead animals, the perfect subjects—while Nollman just jury-rigs some floating drums and paddles out to visit his friends. Can we generalize such a practice? I think so.

Again: "vitality and vibrancy" lie in such details. *All* of the constructive argument lies in such details. It is only by recounting and connecting innumerable stories that the possibilities in front of us, and their perils and their promise, can be seen for what they are. And this, I want to suggest, is truly "deep ecology," whatever else some philosophers mean by that phrase. The "depth" we seek is not some sort of privileged metaphysical profundity. It lies in learning and then inhabiting the infinity of stories and possibilities and connections that open up once you actually find yourself anywhere in this dancing, piercing world. We look not down but *around*. We seek not some philosophical "grounding" but the actual ground: the Earth. We seek "depth" in, as it were, thickness. Let the librarians, when this book must be catalogued in relation to "deep ecological" works now in vogue, call it a work of *"thick* ecology." And so we come back to Earth. . . .

2

Animals Next to Us

My baby daughter is once again pursuing the more disagreeable of our cats as fast as her newly acquired crawl can carry her. Animals in general seem to be one of her innate tastes. From the start she has been absolutely fascinated. The cat's response is more measured; maybe we need a kitten.

My daughter has no illusions that the cat is another human or another small creature like herself. The cat fascinates as a *cat:* as a foreign being, also as a being with some unpredictability and depth. She knows already that this is something quite unlike her toys. She knows that this is a live creature, and thus in a strange way kin, even though wildly different.

My daughter is in no way distinctive in this. On the contrary, the fascination of all children with other animals is usually so obvious as to go unremarked. But for our purposes the fact is striking and central. In our very own beginnings, before we acquired the various prejudices and inhibitions whose uneasy dominance defines "growing up," we already knew a world of connection to other creatures. Children, reports Freud, "show no trace of that arrogance which urges adult civilized men to draw a hard-and-fast line between their own nature and that of all other animals. . . . Uninhibited as they are in the avowal of their bodily needs, they no doubt feel themselves more akin to animals than to their elders."[1] Even for adults, it is not as though a sense of connection to other creatures must be laboriously constructed in some kind of void. For most of us, it is more a matter of recovery of the more-than-human worlds that already lie all around and within our own.

Evolution, according to some theories, often proceeds not by carrying farther the developmental pattern of the "old" species but in just the opposite way: by prolonging certain infantile characteristics of the "old" species into the adulthood of the new. Thus certain forms have become permanent in humans that are only transitional in other primates: relatively overdeveloped brains, obviously, but also infantile behavior, most notably *play*, in all its forms, including singing, dancing, imitation, and making things for pleasure. Some of our fascination with other animals surely arises from this very playfulness. Moreover, the same kind of evolution-by-devolution appears to underlie some other animals' fascination with *us*. The ethologist Konrad Lorenz points out that the domestication of the dog also involves the retention of initially juvenile forms into adult stages. "The ardent affection which wild canine youngsters show for their mother and which in [wild dogs] disappears completely after they reach maturity, is preserved as a permanent mental trait of all highly domesticated dogs. What originally was love for the mother is transformed into love for a human master."[2] Even the dog's bark may be explained in this way. Noting that the dog's wild ancestors bark very little if at all, some researchers now claim that barking is a juvenile trait preserved into adulthood in domestic dogs. "Dogs are really four-legged teens, researchers say"[3]—so the headline blares; but they're *serious*.

Most of the time the remarkable loyalty of dogs is just another familiar fact we do not find at all surprising. We only forget it on certain official occasions, when we go on as if humans constitute the only possible sources of companionship or centers of moral awareness in the world. Once again knowing all along, in some other compartment of our lives, that we are not only not the only examples but probably not even the best examples. The great Jewish philosopher Emmanuel Levinas writes about a dog who strayed into the Nazi concentration camp where Levinas and his fellow prisoners were daily being treated as less than human, as dirt. Every morning the dog greeted them with wagging tail as they were being marched out to work; every night he barked excitedly for their return. The *dog* at least treated them like human beings. Levinas calls that dog "the last Kantian in Nazi Germany."[4]

But others know more of these matters than I. In the great divide between dog people and cat people, I am with the cats. What I want to note here, instead, is the very existence of such a divide itself. It is another one of those commonplaces almost never remarked upon, yet revealing once looked in the face. Philosopher Mary Midgley remarks that the species barrier is like a fence that is very impressive in its upper reaches, insuperable to dressed-up adults "engaged in statesmanlike interactions," but entirely porous beneath, where children and the young of other species scurry through all the time. But perhaps it is not even so insuperable higher up, if most people who have known cats and dogs unhesitatingly identify themselves as "dog people" or "cat people" whenever someone of the opposite persuasion happens by. Scratch the surface of our official species-exclusivism and something quite different emerges.

Cats, anyway, have minds of their own. Dogs have too fully identified with us. No cat would think of sitting all day waiting and hoping for nothing but the return of the master, even if only for a ten-minute walk. No matter how intensely desired your return home is, a self-possessed cat (perhaps that's it: cats have self-possession) will feign indifference when you actually do arrive. Only after a few yawns and a leisurely turn around the house does the question of, say, food come up.

Or perhaps cats really are indifferent and are only pretending to pretend not to notice. At any rate, it is this very enigmatic depth that is fascinating about cats. Compare the overtones of "catty" with "doggy" as an adjective describing people: to be doggy is to fawn, but the catty are *tricky*. More broadly, the possibility of deception goes hand in hand with a general kind of exchange and negotiation between cat and human. Cats have lives of their own, in which we are included, or made to feel included, almost by a kind of indulgence. (Kipling: "For I am the cat who walks by himself, and all places are alike to me.") Cats wish us to know that as far as they are concerned, they live with us voluntarily and only as a relation between equals. However much this may be a proverbial matter of fond sentimentality among "cat people," that feeling has a real basis.

And finally about cats: it is worth noting that very few kinds of cats can be "tamed" at all. Lions, tigers, panthers are only barely domesticable. All domestic cats are descended from one group of Egyptian cats, itself not tamed until about 1600 B.C. Perhaps only then were they discovered, or perhaps only then did a mutation occur that opened the possibility of sociability. Even these cats cannot be trained in the way that dogs and many other animals can be, for use in the circus, for example. Vicki Hearne reports overhearing a venerable professor telling a young researcher, "Don't use cats, they'll screw up your data."[5] Deliberately refusing to do what the researcher or technician wants, for example. Still, as Hearne also points out, the conclusion is not that cats are perverse but that "getting it right," doing things with a kind of harmony and elegance—and with a certain basic respect on both sides—is as vital to them as it should be to us. When we get it wrong, they pull out.

Hearne is actually a "dog person," or rather, a dog and horse person, in fact a dog and horse trainer. Her writing is in part a defense of animal training as what she explicitly calls a moral enterprise: not, however, as the moralization of an animal, but rather the co-evolution or co-constitution of a joint morality by trainer and animal. Correspondingly, she catalogs some of the ways in which humans can betray an animal's trust, for example by refusing to believe the animal when the animal knows better than we do. "Thinking too much," like the tracker who pulled his dog away from the lead the dog emphatically suggested because it seemed to the trainer that no one could possibly be hiding where the dog pointed. But the dog was right. Most fundamentally, we betray animals' trust by refusing to consider that we live in relations of trust with them in the first place. Such blatantly dissonant treatment of another human leads to craziness; there is no reason to think it is any different with other animals.

For us natives of late twentieth-century urban culture, cats and dogs (and for the rich, horses) are almost the only animals we are likely to come to know at all. Yet historically humans have lived with a much wider range of creatures. Cormorants fished for our ancestors; mongoose and falcons as well as dogs hunted; honeybees have been kept since Roman times, answering the bells and whistles of their keepers.[6] Native Americans kept beavers and raccoons, preferring them even to dogs.[7] A. M. Beck reports—can this be true?—that there are 1.8 million pet raccoons in America today.[8] Other Native Americans tamed moose and bear; Brazilian Indian children decorate their pet cormorants; South Asians kept fruit bats, lizards, eels.[9] Keith Thomas reports that animals were literally everywhere in the English towns of the early modern period. Families slept with their livestock, horses were kept indoors, and birds were reared in townhouse bedrooms.[10] Look at the design of medieval European houses: people lived with their pigs. Go to any county fair in farm country; in a sense, some of us still do.

Of course, something was usually expected of these animals in return: they were not the "luxuries" that our pets have now become. Even so, they did not live with us in the way that our domestic machinery "lives" with us, like our vacuum cleaners or bicycles or hay balers. Midgley:

> If people had viewed them like this [as machines], domestication could probably never have worked. The animals, with the best will in the world, could not have reacted like machines. They became tame, not just through fear . . . , but because they were able to form individual bonds with those who tamed them by coming to understand the social signals addressed to them. They were able to do this, not only because the people taming them were social beings, but because they themselves were so as well.[11]

On medieval sailing ships, Keith Thomas reports, dogs and cats were considered "so much a recognized part of the crew that the first Statute of Westminster ruled that a vessel was technically not abandoned as long as either animal remained aboard."[12]

The result was a genuinely co-inhabited world, what Midgley calls "mixed communities," mixing humans and other creatures. And again it is crucial to stress that such "individual bonds" were not formed just out of expediency but rested as well, even often primarily, on a sense of communality and affection. As Midgley argues, mixed communities have a profound moral dimension as well. When the prophet Nathan wants to condemn King David for his treatment of Bathsheba's husband Uriah, Nathan tells the king the tale of a poor man who "had nothing save one little ewe ram, which he had bought and nourished up; and it grew up together with him, and with his children; it did eat of his own morsel, and drank of his own cup, and lay in his bosom, and was to him as a daughter."[13] When Nathan tells David how the rich man stole the lamb to kill it for a feast, rather than take one of his own extensive flock, he knows very well that David will respond with horror and moral condemnation—thereby, of course, condemning himself—

rather than just complaining that people oughtn't make pets out of lambs or feed them from their own cups in the first place. That the lamb lives with the poor family as a daughter is not regarded as strange, or as somehow usurping the potential place of a human child; and the killing of *that* lamb is regarded as *obviously* a violation of something that would not be violated if the rich man killed one of his own lambs, though the lambs "in themselves" might be entirely comparable.

Again, we are speaking of a sense of relation and connection that, despite a good deal of conditioning in the other direction, still is perfectly recognizable even in cases far from our own experience. Few of us adopt lambs in this way, but close modern parallels to Nathan's "rich man's" act, such as the stealing of house pets for laboratory experiments (and, more commonly, the removal of lost house pets from pounds for the same purpose), strikes us as heinous in the same way. It is not merely the animal that is violated. Though that is bad enough, it is true even of the homeless animals in pounds. What is also violated is a community of which we too are parts. The appropriate analogy is not something like stealing a child's bicycle, but rather, as Nathan reminds us, stealing children themselves.

Again too, we are not just speaking of lambs, cats, or dogs, friendly little furry things.

> Working elephants can still only be handled by mahouts who live in close and life-long one-to-one relations with them. Each mahout treats his elephant, not like a tractor, but like a basically benevolent if often tiresome uncle, whose moods must be understood and handled very much like those of a human colleague. . . . If they were [misinterpreting the elephant's] basic everyday feelings—about whether their elephant is pleased, annoyed, frightened, excited, tired, sore, suspicious, or angry—they would not only be out of business, they would often simply be dead.[14]

These relations are one-to-one and lifelong. Even more strikingly, a relational language is absolutely essential to describe them. The elephant is an "uncle": not even an unrelated employee or co-worker, but *family*. Elephants are not working *for* the mahouts but *with* them.

Those who find elephant uncles too exotic may not even know what to make of the experiences of Konrad Lorenz with wild jackdaws, geese, and cockatoos—and this in twentieth-century Austria, of all places. All manner of wild birds lived with Lorenz, inhabited or visited his house, and accompanied him on his walks. He raised several generations of jackdaws, who then anchored (and literally sheperded) many more generations, who lived, sometimes, in his aviary and under his eaves. Lorenz could identify them by their facial features—it just requires paying attention, he said—and could identify *with* them so thoroughly that he himself commented on the relative desirability of the various debutantes one year. ("She was obviously the fairest of the available virgins," he says of one young female, and "had I been a jackdaw I would have chosen her myself.")[15] They in turn preen his eyelids with their beaks in his study. They feed him, with "finely minced worm, generously mixed with jackdaw saliva," which they will force into his ear if he refuses his mouth, pushed in with the beak just as an adult will feed its chicks or a courting male will feed a female. They attempt to entice him to mate with them in tiny nesting cavities—in one case, in his own pocket.[16] Sometimes it is a matter of "imprinting" (a creature's determination of what kind of creature it is, and thus who it might feed or mate with, is sometimes a function of who it *sees* at crucial moments when very young—this is one of Lorenz's most famous discoveries, made when he became father, or mother, to the young of greylag geese). Other times, it is genuinely a matter of Lorenz having become, say, an honorary jackdaw. The animals are not confused at all.

Once again we are reminded of the truly astonishing possibilities for community with the other life that in fact surrounds us at every moment. Lorenz does not go into the jungle to seek out the most exotic or the most humanlike creatures. Look up from your book, right now: there are birds flying and calling outside the window. It is not impossible to imagine that even we might come to understand bird calls and flight patterns as expressive and meaningful, rather than the random or simple-purposive behavior we usually imagine, if we notice them at all. Lorenz just patiently and humbly begins to respond—to the crows. Another biblical connection: King Solomon was renowned for speaking with the birds. Native Americans did so too. One of our oldest and most widespread myths tells of a Golden Age when humans and other animals could converse. Only why suppose that *they* all spoke *our* languages? Or that we know in advance what their "speaking" might amount to? Are we really to suppose that Solomon spoke Hebrew to the herons? Lorenz, at any rate, "speaks" jackdaw. Consciously, carefully, he joins their expressive system.

All of these are open possibilities. That world that seems to us to lie at such a distance, or in which we are so disinterested, is a living, layered realm through which we walk like the deaf and dumb. Who are we even to begin to say what is or is not possible?

When Robert Cushman Murphy visited the island of South Trinidad in 1913 with a party from the brig *Daisy*, terns alighted on the heads of the men in the whaleboat and peered inquiringly into their faces. Albatrosses on Laysan, whose habits include wonderful ceremonial dances, allowed naturalists to walk among their colonies and responded with a grave bow to similar polite greetings from the visitors. When the British ornithologist David Lack visited the Galápagos Islands, a century after Darwin, he found that the hawks allowed themselves to be touched, and the flycatchers tried to remove hair from the heads of the men for nesting material.[17]

Darwin himself, in *The Voyage of the Beagle*, repeatedly marvels at the tameness of island birds.[18] Annie Dillard returns to the Galápagos in our own time, half a century after Lack and a century and a half after Darwin; still

> the animals are tame. . . . You pass among them as though you were wind, spindrift, sunlight, leaves. On Hood Island I sat beside a nesting waved albatross while a mockingbird scratched in my hair, another mockingbird jabbed at my fingernail, and a third mockingbird made an exquisite progression of pokes at my bare feet up the long series of eyelets in my basketball shoes.
>
> The marine iguanas are tame. One settler, Carl Angermeyer, built his house on the site of a marine iguana colony. The grey iguanas, instead of moving out, moved up on the roof, which is corrugated steel. Twice daily, on the patio, Angermeyer feeds them a mixture of boiled rice and tuna fish from a plastic basin. Their names are all, unaccountably, Annie. Angermeyer beats on the basin with a long-handled spoon, calling "Here AnnieAnnieAnnie Annie"—and the spiny reptiles, fifty or sixty strong, click along the steel roof, finger their way down the lava boulder and mortar walls, and swarm around his bare legs to elbow in the basin and to be elbowed out again smeared with a mash of boiled rice on their bellies and on their protuberant, black, plated lips.[19]

She reports that the hawks are still tame. The sea lions are tame: they join the humans on the rocks and try to entice them to play. Dillard's comment mirrors Midgley: "To say that they come to play with you is not especially anthropomorphic. Animals play."

But to say that the animals are "tame" is also not quite right. It is not as though someone has "tamed" them, taken from them their wildness or enforced some sort of discipline. These are open and free offerings. They are part of the animals' very wildness. It is more as if, once again, we look here at *open possibilities*. These animals are willing to approach us with a certain amount of trust and (for some) invitation—as long as we merit the trust and, at least sometimes, accept the invitations. Which also requires that we recognize the invitations as invitations in the first place, and are not oblivious or unbelieving or untrusting ourselves.

Disbelief, still, abounds. Raised with only a passing acquaintance with other animals, many of us cannot imagine any real relation of trust between us and them. Many of us are professionally or ideologically committed to the view that other animals are incapable of being "uncles," really; in fact, incapable of any sort of moral relationship at all. Cat lovers, on this view, I guess, are just dupes, Lorenz a gullible fool. Angermeyer is only oiling his machines. The iguanas even *look* like machines.

It is already clear, though, even from the little that has so far been said, that such relationships exist. For most of human history they have been the predominant form of the human relation to other animals, the predominant contexts and even preconditions of human life itself. The skeptic, moreover, is almost always someone who is actually in no position at all to *know* what is possible, someone who in fact often has a vested interest in *not* knowing. I have heard the greatest nonsense about other animals from world-class scholars who never once looked an animal in the eye or even, apparently, bothered to investigate empirically the prejudices they carry on with such confidence. Animals (they say) don't feel, don't have beliefs, can't play, blunder about—in sharp contrast, apparently, to the exquisitely well-adapted human behavior we see all around us. In fact, as we know in our better moments, it is usually the animals who are exquisitely well adapted, except perhaps in artificial situations that we concoct for them, and *we* who are too often poorly fitted even to the environments we have created for ourselves.

Animals don't play? Julian Huxley described ducks shooting the rapids over a sand bar in Iceland, then waddling back to do it again and again. Ecologist Lawrence Slobodkin describes Kenyan elephants spraying and splashing each other at a waterhole "like stout children at a crowded municipal swimming beach."[20] Everyone knows, when we care to remember, that cats and dogs (and horses and others) can play almost constantly. Birds gambol in the winds. There's an issue of tempo here too. A field researcher writes of the whales: "Everything the whales do is so slow, so deliberate, outside the normal time sense of the human world. When you watch whales for an entire afternoon, you don't realize what they're doing. You see things that look very slow and graceful. Only later, when you've looked at your day's notes, might you put it together and say "Oh my God, this animal was *playing*. . . . Whales teach us a new sense of time."[21] Of course, those of us who never look back in this way may never notice the play at all. Perhaps, one way or another, this is most of us. How many of us are willing even to imagine trying to see things on whale time? But if we do not, how dare we pass judgment in such confidence on what they are or are not doing?

Animals play together. Oria Douglas-Hamilton writes from her elephant-watching hideout at the Ndala River in Kenya:

> Only when the baboons came to the river was it safe for the shy bush-buck to come out of hiding and drink. They know then that there are no dangerous predators around. It took no more than ten minutes for the baboons to settle down, then a twig would crack and through the leaves on the opposite bank I would spot part of a face or an eye, and delicately a bush-buck would appear, and wander past the baboons into the shallow water. One or two more would follow, then they would frolic and play with the baboons. Impalas also arrived nearly every day with the baboons, walking up in big golden herds with their ears twitching ceaselessly. . . . Some days the river was filled with elephants, buck of all kinds, baboons, blue monkeys; even the two rhinos who lived in the Ndala valley would come out or a giraffe might slowly drift along in

the haze of the sand heat. It looked as if all the animals had agreed to spend a morning on the beach, playing, washing, drinking, and sunning themselves.[22]

No one wants to say that animals' capacities are exactly the same as humans. But what exactly those capacities are is very much an open question. "Not exactly the same" does not mean "lesser," either. There are many ways in which other animals are vastly *more* capable than humans; and even with respect to our vaunted intelligence we may now have our doubts, with whales for example singing the same *Odyssey*-length "songs" to each other across entire oceans, these mammals who eons ago returned to the sea and who corresponding have both the tripartite mammalian brain that we do (but larger) and in addition a fourth region utterly impenetrable to us.[23]

"Well of course we do know that intelligence is not directly proportional to brain size, so none of this proves that whales or other cetaceans might somehow turn out to be 'smarter' than us." It is not pointless to question their intelligence. But the question is at least open: that we shall finally win even at our own game is not guaranteed. Intelligence appears to correlate with a number of features of brain structure, such as the number of layers and general area of the neocortex, the degree of folding of the cortical surface, and the degree of regional specialization. Dolphin brains surpass human brains on all these counts.[24]

It *is* pointless to suppose that their intelligence is the same *kind* as ours. "So why don't they use those big brains for something, if they're so bright?" Perhaps it is only that *we* are not bright enough, or sensitive enough, to understand what they are doing. Clearly a creature that evolved underwater, communicating almost solely by sound, able to "see" by sound literally inside each other, with few natural enemies, would use its intelligence in a very different way than a species like us, always in danger, dexterous, closed off by the skin, a tool user early on. Who knows what they're doing with all that brain? Carl Sagan:

> Is it possible that the intelligence of Cetaceans is channeled into the equivalent of epic poetry, history, and elaborate codes of social interaction? Are whales and dolphins like human Homers before the invention of writing, telling of great deeds done in years gone by in the depths and far reaches of the sea? Is there a kind of *Moby Dick* in reverse—a tragedy, from the point of view of a whale, of a compulsive and implacable enemy, of unprovoked attacks by strange wooden and metal beasts plying the seas and laden with humans?[25]

Besides, the worlds even of whale and human do partly intersect; certainly our moral and expressive worlds intersect. That dolphins dance and play both with each other and around humans was known to the Greeks (*Delphi*, named for the dolphins, built above the spot where a dolphin brought Apollo to shore). Dolphins take turns holding a weak or wounded comrade above water. (Like us, cetaceans are air-breathing mammals. Though it seems odd for creatures that spend their lives in the water, they can drown.) They do the same for weak or wounded humans in the water—perhaps making us honorary dolphins, at least extending their sociality to include other social creatures, much as Midgley suggests that dogs, elephants, and many other creatures do as well as us.

So we of the urban West are perhaps beginning to recognize how patronizing and uninformed our views of the other animals actually are. It is unlikely that some of the classics could still be written, like this gem written in 1908, before (as Midgley puts it) "certain embarrassments descended on the human side of the argument":

> In the lower stages of culture, whether they be found in races which are, as a whole, below the European level, or in the

uncultured portion of civilized communities, the distinction between men and animals is not adequately, if at all, recognized. . . .
The savage . . . attributes to the animal a vastly more complex set of
thoughts and feelings, and a much greater range of knowledge and
power, than it actually possesses.[26]

The racism and smug self-satisfaction of this view of non-Europe-
ans is now painfully evident, though there are certainly people
who still subscribe to it, at least in private. But that the suggested
view of other animals is equally smug and unfounded is not yet so
clear. People still believe this sort of thing, even—in fact, especially—people who live in absolute ignorance of the actual capacities of other animals, since that is most of us. A little modesty
would be more becoming. I do not mean that the "savages" are
always right. I do mean that nearly always, as Midgley puts it,
"Western urban thought [is] (not surprisingly) often even more
ill-informed than local superstition on many such questions, and
[has] consistently attributed to animals a vastly *less* complex set of
thoughts and feelings, and a much smaller range of knowledge
and power, than they actually possess."[27] One of my city-bred
friends, pressed on the question why more feminists are not
ecofeminists, denied that real relationships are possible with most
animals. Rolling her eyes: "Do you really think I can have a
relationship with a chicken?" Well, actually, yes. Any child who
has grown up on a farm knows as much.

The psychoanalysis of this skepticism, this denial, belongs
somewhere else. But we oughtn't allow it to escape scrutiny
entirely just because it has so effectively put the chickens and the
whales on the defensive. Certainly other animals are at times
overrated; sometimes because we tend to be very impressed by
parallels between their behavior and ours—so impressed are we
with our own. But what is happening for the animal may be very
different. We cannot imagine capacities or senses other than our

own, so we speak of, and then mock, the "extrasensory". More likely, other animals are just far better tuned and responsive to their senses. "Everyone who understands dogs," says Lorenz, "knows with what almost uncanny certitude a faithful dog recognizes in its master whether the latter is leaving the room for some reason uninteresting to his pet, or whether the longed-for daily walk is pending."[28] Telepathy? Perhaps it would have to be—in us. In dogs, whose senses and sensitivity to mood are far more exquisitely tuned than ours, it is no mystery.

Horses have similar capacities. The case of "Clever Hans," for example, is taken as a textbook example of fakery or trickery. Clever Hans was a horse who appeared to have the most astonishing abilities to understand complex questions asked in human language, to do arithmetic, and so on. At length it was discovered that Hans was actually very good at reading subtle, unconscious signs from his keeper. Questioners would pose questions and then offer Hans a set of choices for the answers, or pose arithmetical questions and expect him to nod the appropriate number of times. Hans's keeper, present through all of this, or sometimes the questioners themselves, apparently would change, become more tense or subtly expectant, when the right answer appeared. Hans recognized this change and stopped. When his keeper did not know the answer, or was not present, Hans floundered and failed the question.[29]

No doubt the hardheads were pleased to discover that horses could not do arithmetic. But overlooked in all of this was an exquisite sensitivity and responsiveness on the part of the horse. And to discover that it is "only" a matter of exquisite sensitivity is surely not to discover a "trick." What we discover is only that we have once again reduced the animal to human models and limits. Responsiveness, not the ability to to do mathematics, is the great virtue of the horse. Would that *we* were so responsive! And responsiveness, once again, is centrally a possibility of relationship. Vicki Hearne argues that it is the precise attunement of horse and rider that makes great horsemanship and horse performance possible. But it is precisely this that is pushed out of focus when purely human abilities are the only abilities celebrated or looked for. Hans was construed as a hoax because he was construed as a pretender to (a certain particular kind of) human status. His actual possibilities were never of interest to the hardheads. The skeptic does not ask what might be made of the animal's real capacities; he only sighs in relief when it turns out that the animal does not challenge his own most vaunted capacities. There is a suspicion, almost fear, of the animal here that underlies the determination not to be "hoaxed." Hence we also reconstruct the animals and their settings so that the unexpected is even less likely to emerge. In the end we may even succeed in reducing the animals to what we imagined they were—a theme to which Chapter 5 returns.

Not to mention that sometimes the animals' own possibilities, like our own, can emerge only when we are in partnership with each other—as Hearne's example of horse riding suggests, and, perhaps more clearly, as dogs' scent tracking suggests. The tracking ability of the right dog with the right handler is truly incredible. In U.S. Army research, whole fields were sprayed with gas and burned after a scent track was laid by humans. Track layers were picked up in cars and moved several hundred yards before continuing the trail, or entered a river and swam downstream underwater with snorkels before continuing on the other side. None of these measures consistently defeated the dogs. Only human obtuseness did that, as when handlers stopped listening and responding to the dogs. The right handler, though, is indispensable. In effective tracking, a dog and a human work together, and though at times either one's preconceptions may get in the way, both are actually vital. The incredible capacity is a *joint* one that does not break down into parts. But of course this no more redounds to the exclusive credit of the human than it does to the dog's.

Specialization within the dog–human relationship may even have influenced human evolution. Maybe relying on the dog's nose freed us up for other kinds of attention. In any case, it pays to remember that human–animal partnerships are not merely personal and passing events in the present but stretch back historically, in fact beyond the view of history itself and into evolutionary time. We have very visibly shaped the evolution of the dog: why mightn't the dog have shaped us, too?

So much more could be said! Paul Shepard argues that a world of animals is necessary to the very development of human thinking as we know it. Animals are crucial to our dreams, to our art, to the development even of categorical language: in short, to the very core of human imagination. We understand ourselves in animal terms: we flounder, we horse around, we doggedly hawk our wares. Etymologically the word "flash," as in "flash of inspiration," comes not from lightning but from the flash-splash of a fish. "Ideas do not flash like lightning but rise like trout to caddis flies."[30]

Again, again, again. The first human cave paintings are stylized animals. Animals intertwine with our taboos, being used from the start, as Barry Lopez points out, to derive and illustrate moral fables (though certainly not always benignly for the animals involved—think of wolves). Animal movements inform our own. We think of ourselves moving with animal grace; our children cry out that they will run like a tiger, fly like a bird, jump like a frog. Tai Chi martial arts are modeled on animal movements. Shepard argues that animal taxonomies offer our first and most compelling invitation to categorize.[31] Even the fact that some animals look to us like machines (like Angermeyer's iguanas) should be rethought and reversed. Maybe it is that our machines look like *them*, animal form is so deep within our imagination. Think of the spaceships in *Star Trek:* most of them are *insects.*

The list goes on, and it is a vital one, but the point for the moment is simpler. It turns out not merely that other animals offer multiple possibilities for companionship and connection all around us, but also that we already live within the webwork and legacy of such connections. Learning to live with other animals is not a matter of somehow crossing centuries-old barriers into a new world. It is, instead, to recognize—in the literal sense, to "re-cognize," to re-acknowledge—that we already exist within them, that we can hardly even utter two sentences or spend a night dreaming without invoking them. Our cultural history as well as our evolutionary history is thoroughly shared with other animals. Our minds, our lives, are permeated by animal forms.

3

Animals on the Borderlines

I have spoken so far of experiences open to all of us, of animals with whom we already live in "mixed communities." Even the relationships that Lorenz achieved, fruits of a lifetime not only of observation but of nurturing, were still relationships with "ordinary" creatures, few of them unknown to his ordinary Bavarian neighbors.

But these relationships form only one end of a vast range of possibilities. If "nature" is in many ways far closer to us than we think, even in the cat's glance and the spiderwebs in the corners, there is also a wild world that is much farther from us than we think. There are experiences that are *not* accessible to everyone. Some of them are barely accessible to anyone. Some are more like gifts than the fruits of any amount of labor. Some may be believable only to the rare reader. Many are quickly vanishing, soon to be thrown open to the disbelief of even the most sympathetic.

To study the wild chimpanzees in their own world, Jane Goodall went to Gombe, on the shores of Lake Tanganyika in what is now Tanzania, where mountains rise twenty-five hundred feet steeply from the lakeshore, and the crumpled terrain is curtained with trees and vines. To study the mountain gorillas, Dian Fossey went first to the Congolese mountains and then to the Virunga Mountains in Rwanda, "corrugated, muddy, cold, dark" volcanoes tangled with nettles and six-foot wild celery; she repeatedly broke bones in falls as she climbed them.[1] Once arrived and set up, accompanied only by native guides, they waited. They did not pursue the animals. Goodall placed herself on a prominent rock and let the chimps work out their own relationship to her. Fossey slowly approached groups of gorillas making gorilla noises, slapping and belching greetings. Already their approach was clearly different from the approach that had been the norm among animal researchers: laboratory based, manipulative, interventionist, even when the subjects were chimps and gorillas, these near-relatives of humans. There was (apparently there still is) enormous resistance to even so simple an acknowledgment as naming the study animals (as opposed to numbering: numbers always seem more "objective").[2] Goodall's and Fossey's approach could not be more opposite: they offer their presence, not even supposing that there is any reason that the animals should accept the invitation. They view the animals as individuals with whom they might have relationships.

Immense patience was required. Fossey spent three years habituating the gorillas to her presence before the first tentative touch. But their offerings eventually were accepted. The result is not only a wealth of new knowledge but genuine relationships of a sort not even dreamed of before. Approached in the wild, once their trust was won, Goodall's chimps seemed more like long-lost relatives, where even lack of a common language was not an insuperable barrier. Theirs are lives with complex dynamics, struggles and tragedies and moments of joy. Goodall credits the old matriarch Flo, one of her oldest friends among the chimps, with teaching her how to be a mother. Goodall was first to discover that chimps use tools: pieces of grass, for example, to lure termites out of their nests (no "primitive" behavior, either: even long-time human observers find the lure impossible to duplicate.)[3] But in a certain sense, still, her deepest and most profound discovery is the very possibility of relationship itself. Other researchers who joined her project later, even though they had carefully read Goodall's accounts first, say that they never dreamed that such relationships were possible between themselves and wild animals.[4]

Fossey's work likewise opened up the world of the mountain gorillas, animals that had been seriously studied only once before and then only briefly. The stories and pictures strike deep. Fossey, lying amid the bushes, first being touched by a gorilla. Her profound and passionate loyalty to the gorilla groups she personally knew—so deep a loyalty that it eventually cost her life. She truly "went native," often speaking only gorilla to visitors at her research station. All of this, of course, was held against her, "as if Dian had lost touch with reality, the world of people, rather than attaining a new reality, the world of nonhuman minds."[5] Critics dwelt on Fossey's various personal difficulties and needs, never considering that it might have been precisely this configuration of difficulties and needs that made the most extraordinary achievement, the most extraordinary connection, possible. Fossey, the critics say, was just "too involved:" as if *not* being "involved" would have gotten her anywhere at all.

Work with the apes reveals a rich range of developmental and social processes among families and social groups. Sy Montgomery: "The games of young chimpanzees are almost identical to those played by human children. Chimps will use round fruits as toy balls, and little ones will often pirouette around and around, spinning dizzily with arms out, just the way human children do; they will use sticks to probe imaginary termite mounds, much as children use cups and saucers for imaginary tea-parties."[6] Gorillas sing to themselves and each other when they are happy. All of the great apes mourn their dead. Birute Galdikas, who studies orangutans in Borneo ("orangutan" literally means "people of the forest" in the Malay tongue), watched a mother lose her infant and reports a depth of tenderness and despair that she considers rare even among humans.[7]

Fidelity among the apes is also striking. Adult gorillas are so loyal to their groups that poachers must kill the entire troop to capture the infants sought by foreign zoos. The contrast to humans is ironic. When Dian Fossey pursued a head poacher after a gorilla killing, he abandoned his wives and children to flee his home when she approached; then his wives ran off too. Fossey kidnapped one of his children in order to trade the child back for the gorilla babies.[8]

Communal defense actually characterizes a wide range of animals. Bees and some birds swarm their attackers: think of sparrows mobbing a crow or a hawk. Elephants and musk-ox groups form a tight circle in the face of a threat, the young and the weak inside. Hunters, in fact, play upon precisely this animal loyalty. Commercial alligator whistles mimic the distress cries of the young; any adult who hears the call will come to the rescue, and death.[9] So do many shorebirds; the Eskimo curlew was hunted into extinction, and related shorebirds reduced to near-extinction level, in the same way.[10] Early whalers, before the tools were developed for high-seas whaling, would harpoon an infant whale, tow it alive and struggling to shore, and then kill the extended family, who followed the baby's cries to try to help.[11] Again, these are the practices of hunters, not a group given to sentimentality. You or I, if we talk about animal loyalties or feelings, may be dismissed as merely soft-hearted. But those who must learn animals' ways in order to *kill* them—whose own lives may depend on being able to kill them—for precisely this reason must understand them as profoundly social and loyal creatures. They exploit those very loyalties. Can't be less soft-hearted than that.

Even the most feared predators are in fact profoundly social and loyal creatures. Wolves are extremely fond of the young, especially their own; nuzzling, licking, playing. Even in 1576, when Europeans believed the worst of wolves, a hunting book reported that "if the pups chance to meet their sire or dam anytime after they leave the pack they will fawn upon them and seem in their kind greatly to rejoice".[12] Contrary to folk belief, wolves do not tear or steal food from each other or from the young at kills. Konrad Lorenz speculates that the strikingly benign behavior of wolves around a carcass, and their carefulness for the young, suggests a more highly developed moral sense than in some other animals, whose social structures evolved under less demanding and specific constraints.[13] Speaking of morality of a different kind, it has also been observed that deposed dominant males in captive wolf packs are treated well or ill depending on how well or ill they acted when they were on top.[14] The savagery we see in wolves, observes Farley Mowat, is more likely a reflection of our own.[15]

Wolves are also social beyond their own species. Ravens, in particular, feed on wolf kills, and may in turn lead wolves to their prey. They have a social relation with wolves as well, regularly traveling and even playing with them. Wolf biologist L. David Mech describes the play:

> The birds would dive or jump at a wolf's head or tail and the wolf would duck and then leap at them. Sometimes the ravens chased the wolves, flying just above their heads, and once, a raven waddled to a resting wolf, pecked at its tail, and jumped aside as the wolf snapped at it. When the wolf retaliated by stalking the raven, the bird allowed it within a foot before arising. Then it landed a foot beyond the wolf, and repeated the prank.

Mech sums up:

> The wolf and the raven have reached an adjustment in their relationships such that each creature is rewarded in some way by the presence of the other and that each is fully aware of the other's

capabilities. Both species are extremely social, so they must possess the psychological mechanisms necessary for forming social attachments. Perhaps in some way individuals of each species have included members of the other in their social group and have formed bonds with them.[16]

So "mixed communities" needn't include humans at all. Elephants at Tsavo National Game Park in Kenya have adopted orphaned rhinoceroses, buffalo, even ostriches.[17] Cats and magpies, foxes and hens, cobras and mongooses, pilot whales and dolphins, can not only coexist peaceably but genuinely enjoy one another.[18] Sometimes, like the ravens and the wolves, they work together. Honey-hunting badgers in Kenya are guided to bees' nests by the pantomiming of a bird, called the "African honey guide"; then the badgers leave a fair amount of honey for the bird, which apparently would find it difficult to break into the hive otherwise.[19]

That other animals already live in social relations is surely part of the reason that they can join human communities in the first place. Remember Mech, speaking of crows and wolves, but also in general: "extremely social [species] must possess the psychological mechanisms necessary for forming social attachments." Remember Midgely: "[domestic animals] became tame, not just through fear . . . , but because they were able to form individual bonds with those who tamed them by coming to understand the social signals addressed to them. They were able to do this, not only because the people taming them were social beings, but because they themselves were so as well."

And then what about—the other way around? The "adoption" of humans by wild animals, looked at ethologically, is only one more example of the same phenomenon. The stories have been with us since the supposed wolf child Romulus founded Rome. Linnaeus wrote of nine animal children (sheep children, cow children, bear children, pig children) in 1758. Forty were described before the end of the nineteenth century, and the twentieth century has brought a flood of further reports. A wide range of animals are again involved: wolves repeatedly, but also bears, leopards, a lion, a panther, sheep, elephants, gazelles, pigs. Even *birds:* ostriches and other species.[20]

Two wolf children were discovered by the Reverend J.A.L. Singh in 1920 near Calcutta. Singh and others saw the girls several times with wolves before they were dug out of an ant mound that a wolf group was using for shelter. Two wolf cubs to whom the girls were clinging were sold at market; the adult wolves in the group were shot or chased off. Singh first left the two girls in the care of a man who subsequently abandoned them; then he carted them for an entire week's trip in the bottom of a wagon to an orphanage. At this time one girl was about a year and half old and the other about eight. The younger died at two and a half without ever learning to walk; the older lived another nine years, more humanized but always considered "retarded."[21]

Singh, provoked by this experience, spent a career researching other such cases. Even in 1833 and in India alone, there were many known cases of human children probably adopted by wolves. Not all the reports, of course, are so reliable. It may well be that some of them stem from various underlying, even archetypal preoccupations, exaggerating the stories of lost or mysteriously reappeared children into something quite different. Europe's long and bloody fascination with werewolves probably offers some evidence for this archetypal preoccupation. Some work by psychologist Bruno Bettelheim suggests that that wolflike behavior can appear in the course of childhood autism, even in children who have never been out of the suburbs.[22]

So even Singh's girls could have been abandoned children who stumbled on a wolf den as a place of refuge. Of course, they might also have been abandoned autistic children who precisely for that reason fit well with wolves. If so, their autism at least can't be blamed on the wolves. Both girls' "retardation" may well have been a result of their trauma *after* their capture, or their commitment to the orphanage, where the same high death rates and "retardation" were often simply the result of lack of attention. In any case, it becomes clear that Singh and his associates were not truly concerned with the staggering possibilities of wolf care for humans but with the moral project of rescuing the children from wolfishness—surely not a mood in which the wolves, or wolf–human mixed communities, are likely to be understood better. Their aim was to civilize the children—make them wear clothes, walk upright, attend religious services—even to the point that universal modes of affection are misunderstood and distorted:

> Mrs. Singh gave Kamala a backrub every morning and when Kamala responded by nuzzling her, she would note in her diary that Kamala was beginning to show "human affection." The . . . conceit that such a demonstration of affection is uniquely human is of course silly. The subtler conceit is that it was Mrs. Singh's decision to give Kamala the rubdown. Wolves in captivity routinely solicit scratching and other tactile attention from human beings.[23]

This behavior in turn, as we have seen, reflects their behavior in the wild.

A boy was reported to be living (in 1960, 1963, and 1966) with a group of gazelles in the Spanish Sahara. Jean-Claude Armen, the reporter, hears hints of such a thing in his desert travels. Approaching the group, at length, having seen the boy at a distance, he adopts the same kind of attitude that Goodall and Fossey later modeled: a patient self-offering, an attempt to win the group's trust by deserving it. He lives and sleeps with the gazelle group for months after first contact. He too, like the boy, comes in time to understand some of the incessant signaling (grunts, licks, facial movements, tail twitches, hoof stamping) that goes on among the gazelles. He too joins in the licking and sniffing, of both the boy and the other gazelles. And in this way it begins to seem plausible to him what was wholly implausible before, that a human child could actually grow up "gazelle."[24]

This child, says Armen, could run and leap as fast as the animals. Later, as a bizarre consequence of Armen's discovery, the boy actually had to outrun a U.S. Army jeep to keep his freedom. He had apparently mastered the gazelles' sign system to the point that on Armen's revisit, several years later, he seemed to be one of the leaders of the group of about twenty gazelles with whom he lived (perhaps on account of the high status of his adoptive "mother," with whom he exchanged constant signs of affection on the first visit, but who had vanished, perhaps fallen to jackals, by the second). Armen was committed to leaving the child with the gazelles, both because experience with other such cases shows that such children cannot be successfully reintroduced to human life after the ages of three or four (in 1960 this boy was about ten) and because Armen came to recognize a profound integrity in the boy's life with the gazelles that he was unlikely to be offered by, say, the U.S. Army personnel who set out with helicopters and jeeps to "rescue" him. Another child, this one in the Syrian desert, also supposed to have been raised by gazelles but captured by the Iraqi Army in 1946, had his Achilles tendons cut to put a stop to his repeated, spectacular escapes: jumping out of second-floor windows, for instance, and outdistancing his pursuers through the streets of Damascus.[25] (I am reminded of a line from Spinoza: "No one yet knows what the body can do.")[26]

All of this means in turn that we have only Armen's word for everything he reports. One can remain skeptical. In general, I fear that the question of human children raised by wild animals cannot be judged in any empirically reliable way, because the literature is so thoroughly steeped in self-congratulatory or self-protective conceits, like the Singhs', or in a kind of reactive romanticism, like Armen's. What may be more important here is simply to insist that there is no reason, in principle, why such cross-species adoptions of human children are not possible. There is good reason to think that they *are* possible. This is the crucial point. We and a great many other species are social animals. There are clear cases of cross-species adoptions and mixed communities of other social animals. Human adoptions of other animals—guide animals and "pets" who, for all the psychological peculiarities of pet keeping, can still become genuine companions and members of human families—is universal and known to every schoolchild. We even know, thanks to Lorenz, that other animals can fixate on humans for their identity-formation. Why not, in the very same way, the reverse? Recognizing our profound commonality with other social creatures, and the human practice of border-crossing and living in mixed communities that is so universal as to go unremembered in such discussions, cross-species adoption of humans becomes entirely imaginable.

We *can* conclude that our habitual resistance to the very idea probably says more about us and the limits of our own self-understanding than it does about the social possibilities of gazelles or wolves. Given even those *possibilities,* human actions in this regard seem profoundly narrow-minded, often just blind. In all reports but Armen's, the human was eventually "saved," the adoptive relationship ended, almost always with disastrous results for the children and always with disastrous results for the animals. The wolves found with Singh's wolf girls were shot without a second thought. After their animal foster parents and siblings were murdered or brutally driven off, these children were expected to reintegrate normally into human life. It is no wonder that they failed. Note that this may be evidence not just of their profound traumatization by "rescue," something totally missed by their "rescuers," but also evidence that there are critical periods of development, such that if certain skills are not acquired by a certain age, they are unlikely to be acquired at all. But of course these children acquired *different* traits, more useful to them in their unusual environment, and perhaps very highly developed—but not, all the same, traits that the investigators or "rescuers" were disposed to take very seriously, or even consider possible. As the philosopher Barbara Noske notes, "the animal environment tends to be treated as no social environment whatsoever," to the point that one writer actually remarks about the wolf children of India that "the raising of a human child by a wolf is not in itself of much scientific interest," though "the observable behavior and personality of a child captured from wolves obviously is."[27] Another example: the general category of "wild children" or "feral children" has traditionally included both children raised by other animals and children who grow up in total or severe isolation or confinement—as if being raised by animals is like not being raised at all.

At any rate, such cases are extremes on a continuum, and the argument here does not depend on them. What they do accomplish is to remind us how much wider and wilder is the range of possible human relations to other animals than we usually think. Speculating about the origins of gazelle children, Armen reminds us that in native cultures it is not uncommon for other animals to be used to nurse human babies if the mother's milk is insufficient and no human wet nurse can be found. Sheep, goats, cows, and even gazelles are used in this way by the Moors.[28] Armen speculates that in a few cases children may wander off or be led off by their animal wet nurses. The connection also works the other way around. Native women around the world "often suckle young mammals just as they would their own children: e.g. dogs, monkeys, oppossums, labbas, acouri, deer", also bear and moose in America;[29] this is usually a first step toward taming them. The same practice occurs in the highest civilizations. Fetishized Pekinese dogs during the Manchurian dynasty had human wet nurses.[30]

The last chapter spoke of human–animal "mixed communities" within human culture. There are a multitude of wild cases as well. Brunilde Sismondo Ridgeway offers evidence that Greek children of both sexes rode gentle but not domesticated dolphins in the bays, harbors, and inlets of the ancient Mediterranean. Thus the many legends and myths about dolphin riding (Apollo, saved by the dolphins, founds Delphi) may have had a real basis in fact: they are not mere mythology at all.[31] Dolphins and humans, playing together, wild and free. And it still happens. When I spoke of this one day in class, two of my students reported doing exactly the same thing as children in Florida.

Dolphins fished with the ancient Greeks. Pliny the Elder and the second-century A.D. Greek poet Oppian both describe the elaborate cooperation and courtesies between fishermen and dolphins.[32] Similarly, the same African honey bird that guides badgers to honey also guides humans: the Boran people of Kenya.

> If the Boran are in the mood for honey, they whistle to call the bird. Or, if the bird is hungry for honey, it flies around the Boran, alerting them with its "tirr-tirr-tirr." Then it disappears briefly, apparently to check on the whereabouts of a honeybee nest, and returns to guide them with short flights and repeated calls. When the bird gets to the nest, it flies down to indicate the right spot and changes its call. The Boran break into the nest and take honey; they leave plenty for the bird.[33]

Ornithologists from the Max Planck Institute have studied the Boran–honeybird relationship for years and report that it takes the Boran almost three times as long to find honey without the help of honey birds.

The Boran apparently learned this ritual by watching the birds and the badgers, identifying with the badgers in their need. In general, animal imitation profoundly shapes human culture and practice. From the jungle to the Arctic. Eskimo igloos have many features in common (type of snow used, location, ventilation) with the dens built by female polar bears when they winter alone and pregnant.[34] Moreover,

> the artistic and philosophical evocation of the polar bear by Eskimo and pre-Eskimo cultures leads one to believe that their insight derives from a special affinity with the bear. To an extent, the Eskimo and the polar bear are alike, the lines of their successful adaptation to the Arctic being parallel. The prey of both . . . is the ringed seal. Their hunting methods . . . are strikingly similar. . . . Some groups of Eskimos move off the land and onto the sea ice in winter, like the bears. . . . Both make their living at the edge of the sea ice and along the shore. And both live with the threat of starvation if the seals disappear.[35]

Same need, same lives, shared world. In such situations men and bears become each other's prey as well. But, as Barry Lopez writes, there is a possibility here of a kind of apotheosis that goes far beyond the simple "kill or be killed" of survival. The human fear of being hunted, and actual encounters with bears, "were not simply terrifying moments but . . . moments that kept alive within the culture the overarching presence of a being held in fearful esteem." To encounter the bear, "to meet it with your whole life, was to grapple with something personal. . . . To walk away was to be alive, utterly. To be assured of your own life, and the life of your kind, in a harsh land where life took insight and patience and humor."[36]

Lopez makes the same argument for the Eskimo and the wolves: "it is difficult, and perhaps ultimately pointless, to try to keep the two ideas separated: what the arctic hunter sees in the wolf, and what we see of the wolf in the arctic hunter."[37] Here is a kind of symbiosis too, except slow-motion and wary, but rooted in the same living commonality: "The Nunamiut are a semi-nomadic hunting society . . . who lead lives similar to wolves'. They eat almost the same foods—caribou, some sheep and mouse, berries, not much vegetable matter. The harsh environment requires of them both the same stamina, alertness, cooperativeness, self-assurance, and, possibly, sense of humor to survive. They often hunt caribou in the same way."[38] A hungry wolf, returning to the nonhunting pack ten miles away, carrying food in his mouth, "is besieged with as much affection as the successful Naskapi hunter is by *his* family." Traditionally, wolves and humans often shared hunting grounds and benefited from each other's kills.[39]

Other examples abound, of imitation, learning, and cooperation both ways. Orangutans at Galdikas's camp in Borneo imitate a wide range of human manners and mannerisms. Primatologists discovered Guinaean chimpanzees using stones and anvils for cracking palm seeds, just like the human population of a nearby village.[40] The capacity of human children to imitate other animals is so strong that animal acculturation of human children sometimes occurs even when human adults are also present, and human acculturation of the animal was intended. People who have adopted chimps to raise in a human way along with their own children found instead that their children were becoming chimps.[41] That was, of course, the end of the experiment (a nice illustration of just how disinterested science really is).

Thinking about these matters pushes us back toward even more ultimate questions of borderlines. Humans becoming chimps, humans *becoming* (other) animals? Did I say that? Surely that, at least, is hyperbole? Affinity is one thing, identity another. Even in cases of "adoption," radical, unbridgeable differences remain.

Yes and no. Of course there remained a distinction between Armen's gazelle-boy and the rest of the gazelles. A child raised with chimps would not simply *be* a chimp. But how strenuously we resist the suggestion that the line could be crossed at all—that the human soul is forever distinct! Yet even such a person as Birute Galdikas uses just these words to speak of Dian Fossey crossing the line. Listening to Fossey doing gorilla vocalizations a decade before her death, Galdikas says that she realized even then that "Dian's soul was already tinged and had already merged with the gorillas'."[42] Sy Montgomery suggests that Galdikas, Fossey, and Goodall were drawn to and also took on traits of the specific type of ape they studied: Goodall socially poised like the chimps; Galdikas solitary, elusive, and quiet like the orangutans; and "towering, dark-haired Dian, so often blustering with threat, intensely loyal to her group" like the gorillas.[43] And, moreover, once again, she suggests that Fossey actually crossed the line.

What it means to "cross the line" is certainly not *clear*. Let us just not discount the possibility that the persistence of the theme of "crossing" in mythology and dream might actually have something to tell us. Diverse myths from societies around the world tell of humans actually becoming other animals: the Indians of the Great Basin told of the Grizzly Woman; there is the Crane Woman of the Japanese, Buffalo Woman of the Plains Indians, a Wild Goose Woman legend common across the subarctic.[44] (Notice that these are women: perhaps it is no accident that those Westerners who approach the border most closely are also women.) Totemistic cultures think of other animals, in Joseph Campbell's words, as "co-descendants of the totem ancestors." Crossing the border, then, is no more than keeping up ties with the relatives back home. Native Americans invited and expected animals to enter their dreams and visions; the animal then became part of their *wakan,* their own being and strength.

Modern thought has not completely ignored this sort of mythology. Psychoanalysis makes much of dreams and myths of animals. Almost all of this work, however, reads animals simply as symbols or symptoms of quite different processes, ultimately to be explained in wholly human terms. Human imagination, on this view, takes animals for its own purposes, and those purposes can be read out of it once the literal claims are discounted. No doubt this is sometimes true. But it is also, oddly, only half of the necessary explanation. Left unexplained is why it should have been that animals, or certain animals, should make such apt symbols in the first place. If snakes look like penises, it is also true that penises look like snakes. Why mightn't *snake* fascination be primal, or at least equally important? Shall we who know nothing of these animals conclude without further ado that there is in truth no autonomy or impressiveness to the animal world, that people who lived close to other animals since time out of mind know less about them, really, than we do, who in fact know nothing at all? From the fact that we know nothing, it is just a little odd to conclude that there is nothing to know.

There are many ways of thinking of "the line" as well. Henry Beston, in a famous passage, wrote of other animals as "other nations": "The animal shall not be measured by man. In a world older and more complete than ours, they move finished and complete, gifted with extensions of the senses we have lost or never attained, living by voices we shall never hear. They are not brethren, they are not underlings; they are other nations, caught with ourselves in the net of life, fellow prisoners of the splendor and travail of time."[45] The metaphor is fertile. Supposing that other animals are "other nations," how might we think of the borders? Some nations are bounded all around by oceans, rivers, or mountains: their borders are "natural." But other borders are only conventional. That one cornfield is in Minnesota and the adjoining field in Iowa is ultimately arbitrary. Shall we suppose, then, that the boundaries of human being are like the shores of a vast ocean, across which nothing travels and from which we depart only to fall off the edges of the world? Or more like the conventional lines we draw on maps, useful for owners of cornfields and tax assessors, but having no ultimate basis beyond convention and convenience? At any rate, why may not there be such things at least as foreign nationals, citizens of one nation living in another?[46] Naturalized citizens? Passports, cross-national friendship tours, border disputes, cross-border smuggling?

At the very least we must recognize that some of the territories abutting our own turn out to be rather surprising. We are willing, perhaps, to acknowledge other primates as at least distant relatives. But even what counts as a primate may be surprising. Many borders are not clear. "Mega-bats"—three- or four-foot wing-spanned fruit eaters of the rainforests—turn out to be primates too.[47] (The more familiar, echo-locating, insect-eating "micro-bats" have similar shapes but come from a different evolutionary line.) Age does not distinguish us: turtles, crocodiles, whales, may well live longer. Some spiders live to twenty, older than most of my students. Bats may live to thirty; Canada geese to seventy; macaws to a hundred; some sea turtles to a hundred fifty. Species age is not a human strong point either. Some contemporary animal species are ancient, were already old before there were even flowers. Alligators, cockroaches, crocodiles, herons haven't changed since the dinosaurs. Penguins—in fact, *all* birds, we're now told—*are* dinosaurs.[48]

More familiar and (perhaps) less unsettling is the topic of human–animal "communication." Some official studies are familiar, especially the chimps taught to use American Sign Language (ASL). Koko the gorilla, with a vocabulary of some five hundred words, could swear in ASL ("you dirty bad toilet" was the favorite), adapt the language to new experiences (a stale cookie became a "cookie rock," a mask an "eye hat"; reflecting her identification with her new compatriots, she even called other gorillas "black bugs"), and ask for a kitten for her birthday. She named the kitten herself—"All Ball"—and mourned her when she was killed by a car.[49]

We might see this work in a new and perhaps more useful light if we first remind ourselves that there is and always has been a vast amount of communication going on between animals. Just as many other animals are fundamentally social, creating and sustained social processes that we may, sometimes and with luck, enter into ourselves, so almost all other animals are communicative, again quite in the absence of humans, and it is these larger, ongoing communicative processes that humans may enter, or try to enter, as well as appreciate and understand in their original forms. Recall Armen's remark about how much subtle communication went on among the gazelles, Beston's point about senses that we have lost or never attained. Well-known work by von Frisch on the "waggle dances" of the honeybees suggests that the bees can tell other bees exactly where to find food sources by the ways in which they crawl about over the surface of the honeycomb in total darkness.[50] Researchers think that whales can communicate with each other across whole oceans (several thousand miles before human noise began permeating the waters; at least several hundred miles now), using the irregularities of the ocean floor to amplify their "songs." New "songs" (we are talking about sequences on the order of 10 to 100 million units in length; if they are stories, they are on the scale of *The Odyssey*) have shown up in quick succession among blue whales around the world.[51] Katy Payne, one of the researchers who made this discovery about whales, subsequently also discovered that elephants communicate partly by rumbles too low for humans to hear. The idea came to her, she reports, when she remembered singing the *Saint Matthew Passion* in chapel choir as a youngster, standing by the organ and feeling the rumble of the huge, low pipes.[52]

These examples remind us that "communication" is a vastly more complex and multisensory affair than we predominantly verbal mammals usually take it to be. That point about our verbal preoccupation also bears stressing: there is no reason to expect other animals to have the same sort of pattern. Think of the importance of the "nonverbal" cues we usually recognize even in ourselves. Gould and others have discovered that the *vigor* of the honeybees' dance is one of the key dimensions on which information is conveyed about the desirability of various nesting sites. In general the bees "receive" the others' information by feeling their motions.[53] Fire ants vary the intensity of their pheromone trails depending on the desirability of the food to which they lead.[54] Conversely, some other animals may be much *more* profoundly "verbal" than we are, like whales and other marine mammals, who generally do not see each other at all, and may even be hundreds of miles apart, and therefore truly have only their voices with which to relate. Anyone who has heard whale-song recordings knows their strangely suggestive and yet haunting character, a depth we can sense but can't decipher:

Speaking in storm language,
a humpback, before it blows,
lows a mournful ballad
in the salad-krill sea, murmurs
deep dirges; like a demiurge,
it booms from Erb to Santa Cruz,
bog low, its foghorn a thick liqueur . . .

Dry fingers rub, drag, drub
a taut balloon. Glottal stops. Pops.
Dry fingers resume, then, ringing
skeletal chimes, they ping
and rhyme—villanelles, canticles,
even a Gregorian done on ton tongues

as, trapped below the consciousness
of air, hungry, or wooing,
or lamenting slaughter,
jazzy or appalled,
they beat against the wailing wall
of water, voices all
in the marzipany murk they swim,
invisible but for their songs.[55]

Gregory Bateson speculates that the main function of verbalization among cetaceans is to constitute and reinforce relationship.
In this respect the animals may have to teach *us* language
(although Bateson argues that this is the main function of language even among humans, though we are misled, by our
peculiar propensity for tool using, into reducing language to
subject–object assertions; anyway, either way, *we're* the biological
oddities again).[56] Certainly we would expect "communication"
to be wildly different, and quite likely "richer," among creatures
for whom each others' sounds are virtually the whole universe.
Captive dolphins at first prefer human music to human speech.[57]

Shared lives, in the case of domestic animals, and shared
environments and challenges, in the case of both domestic and
wild animals, also mediate "communication." That farm animals
and labor animals—from horses and dogs to cormorants, ferrets,
and Midgley's elephants—have worked for millennia alongside
and with humans is the clearest possible sign that human-animal
"communication" is the *norm*, an absolute given that no one
would even have thought to question until these forms of cohabitation had been banished from the lives and even memories of the
questioners. In a similar way, even the mythological "secret
languages" of human–animal communication (say, among sor-
cerers and shamans) become much less mysterious. Shared *bodies*
mediate "communication" too. Speaking of animal understand-

ing of human language, for example, a nearly universal claim among oral peoples living close to the land, magician and philosopher David Abram writes:

> It may at first seem bizarre . . . to assume that other animals could understand our human speaking. It is important to discern, however, that in the absence of writing, human discourse is itself far more embodied, far less abstract than it has become in alphabetic society. Meaning, for an oral culture, has not yet forgotten its rootedness in spoken sounds, in bodily gestures—in, that is, the field of expressive, bodily significance that we clearly share with other embodied forms.[58]

Many native peoples hold that humans and animals originally spoke the same language. Even after the fracturing of this language, they add, some of us still can return to it. Shamans are alleged to return to it with some regularity. Mircea Eliade insists that the shamans' "secret language" is in fact "only a return to a more primordial animal language":

> The existence of a specific secret language has been verified among the Lapps, the Ostyak, the Chukchee, the Yakut, and the Tungus. During his trance the Tungus shaman is believed to understand the nature of all language. . . . Very often this secret language is actually the "animal language" or originates in animal cries. In South America the neophyte must learn, during his initiation period, to imitate the voices of animals. The same is true in North America. The Pomo and Menomini shamans, among others, imitate bird songs. During seances among the Yakut, the Yukagir, the Chukchee, and Goldi, the Eskimo, and others, wild animal cries and bird calls are heard.[59]

Of course there are perfectly natural reasons why a humanly invented "secret language" might draw on animal sounds. But shall we so readily explain it all away? Animals do communicate among themselves in their own voices. We know that humans can join this expressive universe in countless small ways: hunters' calls, natives who follow bird calls to track predators or predict the weather, and so on. Why mightn't humans—native peoples who, we must suppose, are already much more profoundly attuned to the larger living world than we can even imagine—enter it in a fuller way?

Still other kinds of "communication," less commonly discussed, go even deeper, perhaps to the heart of an animal's very being. I take up one final example. Neil Evernden notes, like Lorenz, that elaborate systems of social reciprocity and constraint are normal among predatory animals; perhaps because such animals can be so dangerous to each other if understanding goes awry. The result, he argues, is that even between predator and prey there must be far more complex interchanges occurring than we imagine when we think of relentless killers stalking other animals that for them can only be "prey".[60] Barry Lopez speaks of how some animals can suddenly be hunted down without mercy while others walk away unscathed. Hunting wolves do striking things:

> They start to chase an animal and then turn and walk away. . . . They walk on the perimeter of caribou herds seemingly giving warning of their intent to kill. And the prey signals back. The moose trots toward them and the wolves leave. The pronghorn throws up his white rump as a sign to follow. A wounded cow stands up to be seen. And the prey behaves strangely. Caribou rarely use their antlers against the wolf. An ailing moose, who, as far as we know, could send wolves on their way simply by standing his ground, does what is most likely to draw an attack, and what he is least capable of carrying off: he runs.[61]

To explain this behavior, Lopez begins by reminding us of the importance of looks, of stares, between wolves themselves. An intense stare is often used by wolves to communicate with each other, "and wolves also tend to engage strangers—wolf and human—in stares." "I think," Lopez adds, that "what transpires in those moments of staring is an exchange of information between predator and prey that either triggers a chase or defuses the hunt right there." Wolves and prey may remain absolutely still while staring at each other. He calls this the "conversation of death."[62] Evernden speculates:

> What is under discussion is the state of the prey's being. The wolf stares: objectification is inevitable, unless the prey can resist and effectively deny the wolf's accusation. Those eyes shout out "Thing!" But the prey must not let that interpretation bounce back to the wolf. Instead it must show itself a center of existence, a willful presence which asserts its subjectivity and therefore its kinship with the accuser: I am a subject like you.[63]

Lopez concludes that this is one reason why wolves and other predators sometimes indiscriminately kill cows and sheep: domestic animals don't know how to signal back. They don't know the language; they can't assert their subjecthood. "They have had the conversation of death bred out of them." The result is a mute slaughter.

These are conversations that we too may join—sometimes inadvertently. When humans violate or ignore the terms of the "conversation of death," they may find themselves dead too. The larger expressive universe cannot always be ignored without consequence. I have seen pictures recovered from the cameras of tourists who have been attacked by bears. The feeling I get is that when the humans begin to objectify the animals, the animals fight back. Far from revealing the inherent bloodthirstiness or mechanical nature of such animals, these attacks reveal a consuming oafishness and insensitivity on the part of humans. Correspondingly, says Evernden, we need to become able to "see without staring." He suggests that if pictures are taken at all, people use the type of ground-glass lens that requires one to look toward the ground, in effect *bowing* before what we are photographing, rather than the "aggressive, staring stance" of the usual tourist camera.

We will never know the full range of what is possible, never know all that is going on right now all around us. I have only tried to suggest that even the range that opens to us, co-inhabitants of an animal world, is much wilder and more sweeping than we have yet even begun to imagine. The proper response to an emerging sense of the vastness and opacity of "wild connection" is not a (further) retreat into our own small realms of (supposed) transparency. Instead: fascination, interest, humility. Bowing before the mysteries of the world, entering a kind of wild etiquette.

4

The Land Sings

Human sociability links us to other animals, creatures both close to us and wild. But sociability is by no means the whole story. Even at its limits it does not begin to exhaust human participation in the more-than-human. Crucially, unavoidably, there is also human *sensibility*: human perception, human sensation. Through the senses, we are literally at one with more-than-human worlds. Beyond sociability, behind all the forms of human–animal "community," there lies a much vaster and more profound mode of interchange, and even that term is too weak; in the end it is something more like *communion*.[1] Ultimately, to uncover and to re-cover our relation to the land, to the larger enfolding "environment," we must explore the senses themselves.

You are sitting on a couch, perhaps, reading this book. The printed page preoccupies the eye. Yet every few seconds you inhale air that carries the scents of the world around you: the aroma of coffee, your own sweat of the day, the waste products of factories 250 miles away. Maybe the air is prickly with the static of a coming storm—still below the level of consciousness, but the body knows. You feel the couch supporting you; you let your muscles relax, easily forgetting them. You hear the wind, traffic, birds. Even your eyes, however concentrated, will immediately be drawn away if the cat jumps at a fly. Any out-of-order sense stimulus—the coffee beginning to burn, whippoorwills taking up their nightly calls—immediately pulls you away from the page.

Only with the greatest effort can we disconnect even one sense. Floating in an immersion tank at exactly body temperature, we "lose touch"—but then we only render the other senses more acute. Cover your ears and you hear the roars and gurgles of your own body. We can't even keep our eyes shut very long, and even with eyes squeezed shut we can still sense brightness. Taste is with us at every meal, and even when we fast or are hooked up to intravenous fluids we taste the taste of no-taste, the taste of ourselves. Smell is with us at every breath, and that is quite a few: twenty thousand or so backs and forths a day, taking through our bodies 450 cubic feet of air. Visually, light, color, and pattern virtually define our experience at times. Lack of light in the winter months can even produce an official mental illness, Seasonal Affective Disorder.

Sensory *immersion*: that is our life. Think of other animals too. Half of Earth's life lives underwater: literally immersed. "Losing touch" is unimaginable, is death. Sponges, porous and fluid, feel every tiny current in the water. Moles, immersed in the earth, can sense the slightest disturbances; that is how they find worms. Cockroaches are so exquisitely tuned to vibration that they are regularly used by scientists in touch research. Tapeworms are thought to live by touch alone. Even the most armored animals are in fact highly sensitive. Alligators and crocodiles "neck" during courtship; sea turtles enjoy having their shells scratched.[2] Many mammals literally lick their newborns into life. Likewise, human preemies who are massaged gain weight as much as 50 percent faster than unmassaged babies.[3] Mutual touching, grooming, is crucial among primate groups. We're primates too. Diane Ackerman: "touch is so important in emotional situations that we're driven to touch ourselves in the way we'd like someone else to comfort us." We wring our hands, hug ourselves, massage our heads.[4]

Take smell. Wolves map their territories by urine markers, an entire shared landscape of smell.[5] Dogs' scent marks also carry a vast amount of information about physical, emotional, and social condition. Dogs' tracking ability is legendary, and in general dogs seem to trust scent more than sight, responding to humans and other dogs by sight but never being sure until after a good sniff. Experiments suggest that dogs' sense of smell is on the order of one million times as acute as humans'.[6] Moreover, certain peculiarities in the mammalian "wiring" of smell suggest that smells may be perceivable three-dimensional array. Dogs, it seems, do not just register "deer" as a single specific message. They get a sequence of messages from different parts of the deer's body, yielding an analogue of three-dimensional visual images. Even in the dark, then, dogs can recognize the size, shape, and anatomical features of a deer (as well as, through dogs' other attunements to smell, the deer's sex, physical condition, and mood). And we too, it turns out, have brains wired in this fashion: all mammalian brains are wired the same way. Therefore, presumably, we too have the capacity to smell three-dimensionally, holographically as it were, though we do not actually do so, or at least do not seem to ourselves to do so.[7]

Touch, smell, and taste often operate below the level of consciousness. That is one reason why they are so easy to overlook. Studies have found that people who are lightly touched during the course of a social interaction rate the person who touched them as warmer, and treat him or her more honestly, than if they were not touched—but also that they typically do not remember that any touch took place. They deny it.[8] Smell bypasses the higher (well, the more recently evolved) brain almost entirely. Women living in close proximity tend to synchronize their menstrual cycles by smell—sensing, not consciously, a pheromone in sweat.[9] Mothers recognize the smell of their newborns, and babies recognize their mothers the same way. Surgeons are experimenting with giving children bursts of their mothers' odors along with anesthetic during operations. Mothers can identify T-shirts worn by their children by smell alone.[10]

Touch, taste, and smell also unsettle our self-conception as separate and independent beings; that is another reason we overlook them. Or actively repress them. They are too proximate, too primal, too animal. We want to think of ourselves as minds, not bodies; we want some distance. Anthropologist David Howes argues that the rise of individualism in fact *required* the suppression of smells, required the deodorizing of the world. Living in the constant physical interconnection of the smell world would make it impossible to think of ourselves as separate (and discreet, in a double sense) individuals.[11] In any case, the familiar deodorized and sanitized world of our television ads really only arose, along with individualism, among the European upper classes and later bourgeoisie in the mid and late eighteenth century. It is worth remembering how new and culturally specific it really is. Indoor sinks and toilets became widespread only in the twentieth century. Scavenging nightsoil from the streets of European cities— the *streets!*—was big business throughout the nineteenth century. Paris recycled it into city gardens that in the 1850s produced more vegetables and fruits per city resident than in 1980. The smell of graveyards and buried clergy in the churches permeated all medieval cities. People took few or no baths, as contact with water was thought harmful for skin. You lived with your "aura"— according to Ivan Illich, not something visual, but your *smell*— through life. Only with the arrival of the present century did everyone but the poor lose their smells. "Smell became class-specific."[12]

Actually, though, even in the technologically deodorized world, many smells are not truly eliminated. More likely they are just covered up. Our search for a deodorized world really only leads to a less honestly scented one. Even many of the everyday products that are supposedly "scentless" are in fact scented:

soaps, paper products, and the like are scented to mask the chemical odor of their components, usually with musk.[13] Fragrances are added to concrete to combat the "wet cement" smell, added to carpeting to prevent "new carpet" smell, added to perma-press fabrics to cover the smell of resins.[14] Smell—smell of some sort, even if engineered out of consciousness—remains inescapable.

Certain taboos also contribute to the repression of the senses. This is another large subject. The early Christians reacted against the almost unbelievable sensual excesses and orgies of the high-society Romans by condemning the senses wholesale. It was from Christianity's class consciousness, writes Philippa Pullar, "and a pride in poverty and simplicity, that the hatred of the body was born. . . . All agreeable sensations were damned, all harmonies of taste and smell, sound, sight, and feel. . . . Pleasure was synonymous with guilt."[15] The theme stuck: the Puritans even denounced the use of spices as distracting from godliness. Philosophers too took up the theme, for other reasons. Plato made knowing itself a form of *seeing*: seeing with the "mind's eye," not the physical eye. Descartes, at the beginning of the modern age, took the truth of certain ideas to be guaranteed by their clarity and distinctness—visual metaphors, again, appeals to the "mind's eye," as if this were somehow a natural notion. But why not the "mind's nose?" Or the "mind's ear"—the classic pattern, ethnologist George Devereux argues, for the Sedang Moi of Indonesia.[16] John Dewey, commenting on the old philosophical prejudice in favor of vision, argues that sight is in fact a singularly inappropriate metaphor for knowing. Thinking of the completeness and fixity of a whole situation, imagining that we can "see" it in overview, we overlook its uncertainty, its incompleteness, and the ebb and flow of belief and skill in our engagement with it over time. But Dewey's is an uphill battle. "I see what you mean," we say.

Vision, of course, is really a kind of immersion too. We actively seek just such an immersion in movie theaters or art museums, and this too is a profoundly animal impulse. Yet the hypertrophy of vision still obscures and atrophies other forms of sensory immersion. We do not even know what we are missing. Phenomenologist Miriam Hill, studying blind people, argues that blindness, freeing the blind person from the distorting effects of visual "noise"—from, as she puts it, "the clutter of the appearances"—makes the remaining senses more acute.[17] The world becomes richer. Helen Keller reported just this, gently chastising the sighted for self-imposed sensory deprivation. "Touch," for example, she said, "brings the blind many sweet certainties which our more fortunate fellows miss, because their sense of touch is uncultivated. When they look at things, they put their hands in their pockets."[18] Keller enjoyed music by feel; she could tell the difference between cornets and strings just by putting her hands on the radio. She sensed people's work and places they had been by their smells. In a house that smelled like nothing particular to the sighted, she could sense "several layers of odors, left by a succession of families, of plants, of perfumes and draperies."[19] By her own report, all it took was some attention to the sorts of cues that the rest of us tend to call "subtle," if we notice them at all, but which became for her as obvious as a light going on would be for us.

A lesser reality? No. Hill: "both blind and sighted people are in contact with reality, but in different ways. . . . The blind are forced to see the world from another standpoint, but that perspective is not a world of darkness as the seeing prejudicially choose to believe."[20] After all, we don't experience ourselves as "blind" to electromagnetic phenomena or the like, sensory dimensions for which we have no "receptors." That would suppose, impossibly, that we knew what we were missing. No, we simply live open to the world in our own ways.

A lesser reality? The painter Cezanne, who turns out to have been myopic, just "painted what he saw." The result was impressionism. Van Gogh painted what he saw too; much of what he saw may have been caused by changes in his eyes and brain produced by toxic metal poisoning from his paints. But those "effects" are also *there,* gloriously there. As Hill says of the blind, these painters perceive the world differently, but surely not worse. Look at their art. Cezanne and Van Gogh teach us, the normally sighted, to—what?—*see.*

Keller reports sensitivity to some electromagnetic phenomena. She could "smell" the approach of storms, a sense for which we do not even have a name, but which we in fact share with other animals. Current speculation is that it is a sensitivity to the ions escaping from the earth, prior to earthquakes, for example, and other vapors escaping in lowered atmospheric pressure, before storms, when everything is more volatile and the moisture heightens further the sense of smell. Biologist Lyall Watson caps a short history of "dowsing"—the ability of some humans to find underground water almost by "intuition," unaided by any of the approved scientific devices—with the suggestion that we, ourselves a distinct electromagnetic "presence," can "tune" to the magnetic changes produced on the surface by water flowing underground.[21] The electromagnetic upset that precedes storms and earthquakes produces static electricity that makes our hair, like other animals' hair, stand on end. We can tell. The excitement that we attribute to the sights and sounds of a storm may have, at least in part, much different sensory sources.

Wild possibilities begin to show themselves here. It is not just that the familiar five senses have much deeper possibilities than we might have thought. The actual possibilities of the senses— ours or those of other creatures—are not exhausted by the familiar five. Hill speaks of echolocation in the blind, and then of the way in which the senses of hearing, including echolocation, as well as memory and smell, are connected, heightened, and "grow into a style of holistic knowing . . . referred to as *object perception*—the innate but often unfulfilled ability of the body to know of nearby objects, obstacles, and dangers."[22] Even you and I, with our eyes closed, can tell when we are approaching a wall. We can "feel" space, through a kind of hearing—we remember our kinship with the bats—and perhaps by sensing the different rates of flow of air past our face, as the blind actor–musician Tom Sullivan suggests. "Facial vision," he calls it.[23] And who knows what other senses there are? Fish have a variety of electrical sensitivities; a "lateral line organ," for example, runs along their sides and registers the surroundings through differential pressures. Some species have elaborate bioluminescent abilities as well. Butterflies and whales apparently navigate by the Earth's magnetic fields. Many animals possess two separate chemoreceptor organs in the nose. The second or "vomeronasal," system is apparently keyed specifically to pheromones, thus for one thing allowing the males to detect the approach of female "heat" long before it happens.[24] Humans have it too—in utero, at least.

So there are more senses than five, maybe even in us. There are also, in a way, *fewer* senses than five, even in us. Our five are not entirely distinct. Most tastes are really smells; we actually taste only sweet, sour, bitter, and salt. Almost any real experience engages more than one of the five, and our most intense experiences involve all. Think of Hill's account of "object perception:" a "holistic" style of knowing, she says, that links hearing, memory, and smell. Think of running: the ache of your muscles, the flowing, even vertiginous sights and sounds, the pungency of air and sweat, the taste of salt. Is not all experience, like this, only less intense?

Synesthetic perception—perception that synthesizes several or all of the senses—may even be primary, with the separation of the senses only coming later. This was the great phenomenologist

Maurice Merleau-Ponty's view. Start with sight, for example the perception of color; we do not stay there. "In reality," Merleau-Ponty says, "each color, in its inmost depths, is nothing but the inner structure of the thing overtly revealed. The brilliance of gold palpably holds out to us its homogenous composition, and the dull color of wood its heterogenous make-up. One sees the hardness and brittleness of glass, and when, with a tinkling sound, it breaks, this sound is conveyed by the visible glass. . . . The form of a fold in linen or cotton shows us the resilience or dryness of the fiber, the coldness or warmth of the material."[25] The world is one! We *see*—before or without touch—the hardness of glass, the softness of shavings. Likewise we *hear* "the hardness and unevenness of cobbles in the rattle of a carriage:" we hear soft, dull, or sharp sounds. We *feel* the texture of the wood or steel that we bend in our hands, even with eyes closed. Tony Hiss calls this "cross-sensory" or "multisensory" perception: "It's like seeing that shape of the wind through your eyes, ears, and skin; hearing it slap against a distant flagpole, watching it curl through the branches of a nearby tree, and then feeling it land softly on your face."[26] Merleau-Ponty: "Synaesthetic perception is the rule, and we are unaware of it only because scientific knowledge shifts the center of gravity of experience, so that we have unlearned how to see, hear, and . . . feel, in order to deduce, from our bodily organization and the world as the physicist conceives it, what we are to see, hear, and feel."[27] Likewise, Miriam Hill speaks of object perception as a "synergistic blending" of touch, echo, and movement, though if Merleau-Ponty is right, this is to grasp the true phenomenon the wrong way around. For Merleau-Ponty, object perception comes first, then only later is, as it were, *unblended.* Perhaps we ought to say that we really have only *one* sense rather than five, or a multitude of senses rather than a few, where we "count" by situation or activity (running, eating, even sleeping) than by organs.

These thoughts at least begin to suggest how plastic—how changeable, how wildly variable—the senses really are. As in the world of human–animal sociability, the real possibilities may be far more fantastic and varied than we suspect. Striking in the same way are studies of children who grew up in isolation or alone in the woods, such as Kaspar Hauser and Victor of Aveyron. Victor, discovered at about age twelve after at least six years in the woods, had especially highly developed senses of smell and taste. Kaspar Hauser was kept in confinement, probably for the entire first sixteen years of his life, but his senses, instead of being dulled by the experience, were "so sensitive as to be a source of pain to him after he was released into the sensorially overwhelming larger world."[28] Like Victor and like Helen Keller, Kaspar had a highly developed sense of smell. Like them, for instance, he distinguished fruit trees at a distance by smell alone, though unlike Keller, he found most smells unappealing. Both children, as well as Singh's "wolf child" Kamala, had extremely keen senses of hearing. Kaspar could distinguish people at a distance by the sound of their footsteps. Vision for all three was of lesser importance. Victor's gaze was very erratic, Kamala and Kaspar could see very well in the dark but found light painful. Kaspar had "an almost supernatural sense of touch." Touching humans or animals gave him such strong senses of heat or cold that he felt as though he'd been hit. He could distinguish metals by touch alone; he could even determine the orientation of magnets by the delicate air currents that he sensed around them.[29]

After these children were returned to culture as we know it, their senses went through extraordinary changes. The physician Jean Itard, in whose care Victor ended up, stubbornly ignored Victor's sense of smell, even though by Itard's own account smell was by far Victor's most developed sense and therefore (one might suppose) offered the best insights into his mind. Instead, Itard believed that the sense of taste was crucial. For Victor, taste was purely related to food. For Itard, it was a vanguard of "taste" in the intellectual and aesthetic senses, such an important notion for the eighteenth and nineteenth centuries (Victor was captured in 1800). So Itard made great efforts to accustom Victor to French cuisine ("quite clearly the first step in teaching him to become a consumer of the dainties of French civilization").[30] But after Kaspar had been enculturated, in the words of his own enculturator, "the extraordinary, almost preternatural elevation of his senses . . . has sunk almost to the common level. . . . Of the gigantic powers of his memory, not a trace remains."[31]

Could it be that our own senses are equally reduced? What gigantic powers may *we* have lost? Claude Levi-Strauss points out the abilities of some people to recognize vast numbers of different trees and shrubs: 250 by a Seminole Indian; 350 by the Hopi; more than 500 by a Navaho. This in contrast to the urban European American who may not be able to identify any trees or shrubs at all. Sy Montgomery writes of Dayak trackers in Borneo who can "tell you, from looking at bent twigs, which animal passed by here and how long ago, how quickly it was going, and sometimes what brought it here in the first place".[32] Nunamiut hunters escorting even the best American wolf biologists still have to point out nearly everything: subtle variations in coat and behavior, robins picking up wolf hairs as signs of wolf denning and den location. Inuit (Eskimo) in general have far better visual discrimination than Europeans.[33] Inuit at sea in their kayaks navigate through impenetrable fog by listening for the different quail dialects specific to each headland.[34] Andaman Islanders, living in a world full of odors as distinct kinds of trees and lianas come into bloom over the year, organize the year by scents; they have a scent calendar.[35]

Levi-Strauss relates the Navahos' amusement at the inability of an anthropologist to learn a certain aboriginal language because she could not *see* the difference between various plants that the language recognized. Possibly certain powers of observation, like certain expressive responses (again; human, gazelle, or whatever), must develop at definite age–stages or they do not develop at all. Otherwise they may be as mysterious to the non-seer as language to the non-linguistic. Or perhaps they develop differently. Arguably the senses specialize, and specialize differently in different cultures and environments.[36] Who knows, that fabulous capacity to notice a manifold of subtle distinctions may, in us, be diverted into unheard-of channels, may even be applied to commodities—different varieties of tennis shoes, different makes of car—or reconstructed into the ability to make use of elaborate sets of categories, like plots or punchlines of jokes in grade-C movies. This might at least help to explain our obsessiveness about such things. It also suggests that all is not lost: we might once again learn.

The anthropologist Hugh Brody insists that key Inuit terms for intimacy with the land are not translatable at all because they depend so much on a knowledge of *that* land, of hunting on the shifting sea ice under the midnight sun, and also because the very idea of intimacy with the land, *any* land, in the first place seems to have been lost to us.[37] Once again we are in a speculative position, but the least we can do is to resist the inference, from the paucity of translated Inuit terms or the increasing marginalization of Inuit culture, that there is not much to it. Quite the contrary. It may be the very richness and situatedness of their language that resists translation, and leaves their culture so vulnerable to disruption.

A general practitioner working among the Cree in northern Quebec finds the people becoming increasingly agitated one winter when the snows are late in coming. He finally asks why. "His informant seemed to have difficulty framing the answer; the matter seemed so transparent, it was hard to imagine anyone missing it. As it turned out, they were worried about the small burrowing creatures, some of whom would die without the snow's insulating effect."[38] Intimacy: attention to the seasons, their cycles and irregularities; and to the other creatures. The words almost hurt: "the matter seemed so transparent, it was hard to imagine anyone missing it."

Sensory immersion is a kind of given of the so-called primitive life. Remember that Native Americans never viewed this land as a "wilderness," any more than one could view one's own home as somehow forbidding and wild. They knew it too well. Historian Roderick Nash relates that when he was speaking, through an interpreter, to a hunter–gatherer from the Malay jungle, "I tried without success to discuss wilderness. When I asked for an equivalent word I heard things like 'green places,' 'outdoors,' or 'nature.' Finally, in desperation, I asked the interpreter to ask the hunter how he said 'I am lost in the jungle.' An exchange occurred at the conclusion of which the interpreter turned to me and said with a smile that the man had indicated that he did not get lost in the jungle."[39] The jungle, to us wild and hostile, is, for him, home. Just so did Chief Luther Standing Bear, in a beautiful and well-known passage, speak of the American prairies:

> The land was ours to roam. . . . We did not think of the great open plains, the beautiful rolling hills and the winding streams with tangled growth as "wild." Only to the white man was nature a "wilderness" and . . . the land "infested" with "wild" animals and "savage" people. . . . Not until the hairy man from the east came and with brutal frenzy heaped injustices upon us and the families we loved was it "wild" for us. When the very animals of the forest began fleeing from his approach, then it was that for us the "Wild West" began.[40]

Those ideas, wildness and infestation and savagery, and the entire set of valuations that comes with them, were an import from

Europe. Likewise, the Amazonian Indians found it hard even to begin to understand Christianity, with its vision of paradise somewhere else. Paradise was, quite obviously, *right there*. Christians had somehow forgotten how to see it.

We still have no sense of this kind of intimacy. We don't even imagine it possible. We speak without a second thought about such things as the "trackless wilderness," for example, forgetting that humans and other creatures have been "tracking" nearly everywhere for millennia. Gary Snyder:

> One August I was at a pass in the Brooks Range of northern Alaska at the headwaters of the Koyukuk River, a green three-thousand foot tundra pass between the broad ranges, open and gentle, dividing the waters that flow to the Arctic Sea from the Yukon. It is as remote a place as you could be in North America, no roads, and the trails are those made by migrating caribou. Yet this pass has been steadily used by Inupiaq people of the north slope and Athapaskan people of the Yukon as a regular north–south trade route for at least seven thousand years.[41]

In the 1970s, during the debate over the Alaskan national parks, native people felt as though their own inhabitation, their own long-standing communion with and respect for the land, was being pushed into the darkness by the dominant discourse, obscured behind the pervasive talk of the "wild" and the "nothingness of the frontier." As one anthropologist put it, the very idea of "wilderness" in the Alaska debate was "ethnocentric to the point of being insulting."[42] In the end, the Alaska National Interest Lands Conservation Act allowed for native subsistence activities within the new parks—a first in American history. Some native people finally attained legal recognition as part of the land, as members of the larger living community, as "part of the Earth."

Much is lost to us. But there also remain, even for us, cultural resources for a profound sensory immersion in nature. Despite Christianity's devaluation of the senses, they are not absent even in Christian culture itself. Think of Europe's soaring cathedrals and abbeys, the celebrations of feast days, Gregorian chant. Think simply of colors. The monastic Carthusians invented chartreuse; the Benedictine monks named a new shade of dark brown after themselves. Still more enduring are certain texts and images. I do not know what the Puritans made of the book of *Song of Solomon* in their own Holy Book. Some Christian theologians read the *Song* as an allegory of Christ's relation to the Church. Read it straight: it is a love poem dripping with sensory delight.

> Arise, my love, my fair one,
>> and come away;
> for lo, the winter is past,
>> the rain is over and gone . . .

And what comes of that rain! Apples, grapes, pomegranates, nectar, honey, milk, nuts, wine. The voice of the turtledove announces spring; lilies, flowers of all sorts bloom over the hills. We are bathed in smells: smoke, myrrh, frankincense. Doves, goats, ewes, gazelles and hinds of the fields, lions, leopards frolic through. Dews, mountains, springs, orchards; the cedars of Lebanon, slopes of Gilead, Mount Carmel. Nature, in short, is elaborately, lavishly, dizzily celebrated. If the poem is an allegory at all, it is a song of the human immersion in and love for this world. *That* is the real love story.

Solomon's love song; the Song of Songs, as Judaism knows it: the song that somehow contains all songs. The *Song* invokes spring, the end of the rains, thus the cycling of all the seasons: easy-living summer, the brilliance of fall, its excitement and the crispness of the air; the dazzling fairyland of snow- and ice-draped woods. By invoking the "Holy Land" it reminds us that all land might be holy, *is* holy, that our own places may be loved with the same fervor. Think of how many towns in America are named "Gilead," "Mount Horeb," "Lebanon," "Carmel"; our ancestors felt that they were rediscovering holy land. By invoking perfume so persistently, the *Song* reminds us that nearly all the scents we adore come from nature, from flowers, fruits, woods, spices, musk (a substance found in the abdomen of certain East Asian deer), ambergris (amber grease: from the intestines of sperm whales). Jasmine, lily of the valley, rose, sandalwood, cedar, vanilla, civet (made, originally, from the genital secretions of Ethiopian wild cats—it is not clear how humans discovered it, but, as Ackerman remarks, bestiality was not uncommon among sheperds in the desert). Humans can detect musk in amounts as tiny as 0.000000000000032 of an ounce; chemically it is close to human testosterone. A perfumer reports that the "base notes" of perfumes "are almost always of animal origins, ancient emissaries of smell that transport us across woodlands and savannas."[43] Flowers, after all, are the sex organs of plants, reminding us of "all the optimism, expectancy, and passionate bloom of youth."[44]

By singing, just by singing, the "Song" reminds us that we worship—that we respond to and love this world—not just or mainly with our minds, but with our bodies, our voices, our tears. Our poetry. Walt Whitman, surely one of the preeminent modern poets of the senses, links the very awakening of his poet's voice to the sounds of the sea on the beach and the song of a bereft bird:

Out of the cradle endlessly rocking,
Out of the mocking-bird's throat, the musical shuttle,
Out of the Ninth-Month midnight
. . . where the child
   leaving his bed wander'd alone, bareheaded, barefoot
I, chanter of pains and joys . . .
A reminiscence sing.

"Out of the Cradle Endlessly Rocking," part of a cycle of autobiographical sea poems composed in 1858 and reprinted in *Leaves of Grass,* is full of lilac scent and the "white arms of the sea's breakers," and Whitman's beloved Long Island—"Paumanok" to the Algonquian Indians (meaning "whale"; they knew its 150-mile-long shape long before Europeans set out to map it). He is lured back again and again by birdsong: songs of joy and loss; a nesting shorebird has lost his mate, and sings forlornly to her through the night, and finally,

> The aria sinking
> All else continuing, the stars shining,
> The winds blowing, the notes of the bird continuous echoing,
> With angry moans the fierce old mother incessantly moaning . . .
> The yellow half-moon enlarged, sagging down, the face of the sea
>   almost touching,
> The boy ecstatic, with his bare feet the waves, with his hair the
>   atmosphere dallying . . .
>
> Demon or bird! (said the young boy's soul)
> Is it indeed toward your mate that you sing or is it really to me?
> For I, that was a child, my tongue's use sleeping, now I have
>   heard you,
> Now in a moment I know what I am for, I awake . . .[45]

And it is not just that this experience awakens his own voice. His voice mirrors the voices he has been hearing. The poem mimics the rhythms of birdsong, and at the end, fading, the whispers of the sea.

Chapter 1 cited a line of Snyder's: "the original poetry is the sound of running water and the wind in the trees."[46] He means this literally. Poetry—and not just poetry but all of our evocative language, maybe *most* of our language—can be heard as *the voice of nature itself,* whispering, murmuring, rumbling, flashing, booming, gurgling through our own voices. Listen to the onomatopoeia just in those words! The Earth speaks through us, directly. In our own mouths are the sounds of natural places, of streams, storms, lightning; of the birds named for their calls: whippoorwills, chickadees, cuckoos. The last chapter suggests that other animals can sometimes understand and participate in human language. To some extent our language itself may be borrowed from them, from birdsong, for example, and to some extent both our language *and* theirs may be borrowed from the larger enveloping environments that humans and birds have sometimes both shared. Birds may understand us because we speak of the same world—and so may we understand them. As Richard Nelson reports, the hermit thrushes singing in the Koyukon forest thickets at dusk speak the Koyukon words for "it is a fine evening"—or rather, the Koyukon have taken up in their own speech the song the thrushes sing on fine evenings.[47] Nelson goes on to note that the rhythm, the tone, the "feel" of the Koyukon language as a whole seems to be shaped by birdsong.

Human music, as well as our speech, may begin in birdsong— or, who knows, with the omnipresent rhythmic buzzing of the cicadas, all summer, or with the eerie sounds of whalesong echoing up through the hulls of boats, known to sailors since antiquity. Keith Thomas notes that beekeepers as far back as the Romans sang and talked to the bees.[48] And then there is the land itself. On the island of Gomera in the Canaries, people use an ancient whistling language to communicate across their sprawling valleys. "They trill and warble a little like quails and other birds, but more elaborately, and, from as far away as nine miles, they hear one another and converse as their ancestors did. *Silbo Gomero* the idiom is called, and some islanders mix it with Spanish vocabulary to make a creole of whistle and word. They find this hybrid language precise enough."[49] One American parallel, perhaps, is the old Appalachian "holler." "Hollering" itself is probably named for the "hollows" whose sound-funneling it relied on; the hollows themselves perhaps named, again onomatopoeically, for the characteristic reverberations they produce.

So the land itself sings through us, in a sense: not just its creatures, not just its winds, but its own shapes, its rises and falls, its echoing canyons and ragged edges and long sweeping horizons. The valleys, the hollows, shape their own songs too. Australian aboriginal people sing the "songlines:" songs that trace multiple paths through the landscape, describing and guiding by mirroring the land. Bruce Chatwin:

> Regardless of the words, it seems the melodic countour of the song describes the nature of the land over which the song passes. So, if the Lizard-man were dragging his heels across the salt-pans of Lake Eyre, you could expect a succession of long flats, like Chopin's "Funeral March." If he were skipping up and down the MacDonnell escarpments, you'd have a series of arpeggios and glissandos, like Liszt's "Hungarian Rhapsodies."[50]

These are not just songs *about* the land. They are more like musical maps: maps of the land, also cultural maps, sung stories, stories of how the land came to be what it was, how the Dreamtime Beings created and re-created it. Song stories, yet precise enough maps that the Pintjantjatjara people can "sing" strangers to a single stone in an apparently featureless desert. Like Polynesians who could find little speaks of land in the midst of vast oceans by watching the patterns—sea currents, bioluminescence, scents in the wind, keeping track of all of it through *chant*—so the desert songs sing *patterns*: wind and sand patterns, small changes in elevation and vegetation.[51]

Much is lost to us. Not only do we hardly know how to listen to the thrushes; in many places there are no longer thrushes to hear. Yet the Koyukon or the Pintjantjatjara have no different eyes or ears than you or me. We lack the attentiveness, and the kind of culture that informs and deepens it. Yet even this is not impossible for us. These years, consumed by the needs of young children, I am lucky to spend a week a year in the wild, sleeping outside and walking all day. What is always surprising is how little it takes. How quickly the senses reawaken. Attention comes back. Colin Fletcher speaks of backpacking as "remembering that happiness has something to do with simplicity:" removing the distractions and conflicts and dis-integration. Reintegrating the senses,

> by slow degrees, you regain a sense of harmony with everything you move through—rock and soil, plant and tree and cactus, spider and fly and rattlesnake and coyote, drop of rain and racing cloud shadow. After a while you find that you are gathering together the whole untidy but glorious mishmash of sights and sounds and smells and touches and tastes and emotions that tumble through your recent memory. Then you begin to connect these ciphers, one with the other.[52]

The point is not merely that you have sorted out your own head. More, you begin to reconnect to larger living worlds. Even the simplest events become remarkable, stand out. Just walking through the woods on the most ordinary rainy day, the smells and colors can be overwhelming. Sleeping on the earth for more than a night or two gives you a sense of "groundedness" that makes the return to beds uncomfortable. You remember the elements: the pulsations of sunlight finally arcing through the mists of a fall morning campsite, lightning ripping the trees apart at night over your tent, the sudden rise of the wind that warns or delights.

I am learning that the experience is in important ways synesthetic. Merleau-Ponty is right. Hiking magazines are filled with pictures of vistas, and one could easily imagine that the whole aim of the hike is simply to see the mountains, which no doubt explains why it seems so natural to road builders to build "skyline drives" along the great wild ridges. It saves you the trouble of walking. In fact, the vista by itself is nothing. What is crucial is the clear air, the scream of the red-tail, the ache in your legs, the sweat, the sheer *time* it requires to climb up, step by step, feeling the bulk of the mountain as you rise. All of this together. "Alone in the forest," says Jack Turner, "time is less 'dense,' less filled with information; space is very 'close'; smell and hearing and touch reassert themselves. It is keenly sensual. In a true wilderness we are like that much of the time, even in broad daylight. Alert, careful—literally 'full of care.' "[53] Vision retreats to one's dreams, and my dreams, I always find, become more vivid. "The body brings the mind along."[54]

I once took my Ph.D. seminar in the philosophy of nature to a wigwam in Hauppauge, Long Island, New York. Half a mile from the Nothern State Parkway, but we did not hear the cars, perhaps because we were so immensely distant from the parkway and all it stands for, in time if not in space. It was drizzling, foggy, and cold; the mists from our voices rose to join the smoke seeking the small smokehole; we passed a cup, alerted to the calls of geese and wild turkeys—penned, to be sure, but still calling excitedly in the fog. We sat on the ground and talked about Abenaki creation stories. We spoke slowly for once, not covering all other sounds with our voices. And that small matter of tempo in the end may be the best mirror of the intuition the stories spoke of, that sense of being simply part of a larger living world. There was something to hear besides ourselves: the calls of the birds and the wind; our fire echoing the hiss of the rain; and our voices, when we spoke, interweaving among the animals'. *This* is what it means to feel, as Native Americans always said, that "The Earth is Alive." We are speaking of experience, first and foremost, and despite the sound of the language, nothing exotic: experiences that easily could be "right next to us."

This afternoon a storm is brewing and the trees are swinging in the winds, the worried tone of the birds is unmistakable, and even my neighbors, unloading their groceries, feel a note of urgency and suppressed fear and excitement. Here beyond question is a larger world a-stirring, restless. (Lyall Watson: "Without wind, most of Earth would be uninhabitable. The tropics would grow so unbearably hot that nothing could live there, and the rest of the planet would freeze. Moisture, if any existed, would be confined to the oceans. . . . But with the wind, Earth comes truly alive.")[55] We are right in the middle of it. We do not live in cellars, and even if we buried ourselves as securely as we imagine we can bury nuclear wastes, the Earth moves too. Oh, hell: even the *rocks* move.

> There never seems to have been any doubt that Rocks came before living things—that they were, in a sense, the first beings. In the oldest myths Rocks are tricky objects. Sometimes alive, or at least inhabited by spirits, they could move around and turn into other things. Monotheism quieted them down. They became Rocks of Ages, symbols of heavenly permanence and power. . . . Evolution seems to have reversed this trend toward quiescence and Rocks are on the move again. . . . We know that some of them were once alive, that many will be alive again as their elements break down into soil and are taken up by plants, and that they are constantly on the move.[56]

The Sioux thought of rocks as ancient spirits, now semi-retired after producing less enstoned beings. Thoreau experienced the same. Climbing Katahdin, he writes, "I arrived upon a side-hill, where rocks, grey, silent rocks, were the flocks and herds that pastured, chewy a rocky cud at sunset. They looked at me with hard grey eyes, without a bleat or a low."[57] Paleobiology agrees: some now theorize that life itself (or rather, the less enstoned kind) may have begun not in water but in clay. And again, the rocks themselves move, as surely as we and the trees do, only more slowly, or more convulsively. "The whole planet," writes Lyall Watson, " is constantly flexing and stretching." The Earth has tides: the Earth rises and falls, responding like the waters to gravity, centrifugal force, atmospheric pressure and changes, sun and moon.[58] The continents themselves with all their indomitable ranges slide around on molten rock like eight year olds learning to ice skate.

Thoreau also writes of Walden Pond booming in the springtime, as the ice heats up or cools off faster than the underlying water: "Who would have expected so large and thick-skinned a thing to be so sensitive? Yet it has its law to which it thunders obedience when it should as surely as the buds expand in the spring. The earth is all alive and covered with papillae."[59] Walden Pond, like the Earth itself, crackling and rattling across the spectrum. Electronic equipment in a Buddhist temple at Wat Tham Krabok records the electrical phenomena of the Earth, which are written into the traditional eighteen-bar phrases of Thai music and played by the monks on Thai instruments with electronic organ as backup.[60] In REM sleep—dream sleep—our brain waves range betwen eight and thirteen hertz, a frequency at which flickering light can set off epileptic seizures. The Earth itself signs on at around ten hertz. So, in our most fantastic and private moments, we tremble in tune with the Earth.[61]

James Lovelock's now-famous "Gaia Hypothesis" tells us that all life on Earth functions in some ways as a single living thing, functioning so as to maintain relatively stable and optimal conditions for its own continuance. All life on Earth and its processes and detritus, from farting herbivores (producing methane) to coral reefs (which Lovelock thinks help control the salinity of the seas) function in an integrated and self-adjusting way.[62] Surely in some sense this is true, though in *what* sense remains in conten-

tion: "Gaia" is a *hypothesis,* however lyrically and lovingly described, and it has been much reformulated and narrowed as
Lovelock has responded to increasing criticism in recent years.[63]
Perhaps in some very distant way, if true, it may serve as some
kind of confirmation that the Earth is "alive." But let us not
substitute the most indirect scientific speculation for the much
more direct and particular evidence of our senses. One last time: it
is our sensory immersion that most profoundly links us to the
land. Lovelock is making inferences from spectrographic studies
of other planet's atmospheres and hypotheses about the Earth's
early chemistry; and he is talking about the entire Earth and all its
life forms. When you or I say "the Earth is alive," we are watching
the winds dance with first one and then another tree around a
field, or fitfully awakening to a parliament of owls convening
above our tents all night. Lovelock reminds us that the atmosphere is a real, palpable presence, a true ocean in which we live;
a world-swaddling sea that weighs, altogether, 5,000 trillion tons.
But what we know is something more local, its life more heaving
and light-winged. This is *our* air,

> always vibrant and aglow, full of volatile gasses, staggering spores,
> dust, viruses, fungi, and animals, all stirred by a skirling and
> relentless wind. There are active fliers like butterflies, birds, bats,
> and insects, who ply the air roads; and there are passive fliers like
> autumn leaves, pollen, or milkweed pods, which just float. Begin-
> ning at the earth and stretching up in all directions, the sky is the
> thick, twitching realm in which we live. When we say that our
> distant ancestors crawled out onto the land, we forget to add that
> they really moved from one ocean to another, from the upper
> fathoms of water to the deepest fathoms of air.[64]

In truth we live *in* this planet, not *on* it: we swim in the air—and
the air, like the ocean, is itself full of life, and is itself electric. That
is what the senses tell us, or rather open to us, or rather open us *to.*

The world is not "out there" somewhere, channeled in through a few narrow gates or remote videocameras, easily shut off, but *here*, always, all around us, within us, the ocean itself. No sluice gates, no "channels:" *immersion.* That is what it means, finally, to be "part of the Earth."

5

Desolation

We are immersed in this planet: yes. We already live in social relations with any number of other creatures: yes. Yet something else must also be said. All of this is only a shadow of what it once was. Our senses are almost wholly captivated by the relentless geometries of our cities and the flickering imagery of our televisions. Our sociability is almost wholly consumed by our interchange with other humans. How little sense we have, quite literally, of more-than-human worlds! We have come to the point that our own children define "wilderness" as what's under their beds.[1] Compare that to native people, who have no concept of wilderness at all, even in the jungle or under the merciless stars. The Other, denied and destroyed, quite literally comes back to haunt us.

This loss, this turning inward, I shall call "desolation." *Desolation*: literally, driving ourselves into loneliness. Funneling both our sociability and our sensibility into the closed circle of human life alone. Every species lost or driven to the corners, every natural place remade for our purposes, leaves us and our places a little closer to dominating the stage. Every childhood without the woods and the stars leaves them all the more alien, frightful—all the better lost.

The reports of the early Europeans in America, repeatedly attested to by all manner of observers, are now painful to read, hardly imaginable. Ducks, turkey, deer, lynx in awesome abun-

85

dance. Whales so crowding the waters that they were navigational hazards. Cape Cod named for its waters clotted with cod,
salmon running thick in every Atlantic river from Labrador to the
Hudson. Lobsters so common that they were used throughout
New England for potato fertilizer, pig food, and fish bait; British
sailors rioted when forced to eat lobster more than three times a
week. Islands that were once packed shore to shore with walrus
or seals or nesting seabirds are now empty. The spearbill, just for
one, is now extinct, slaughtered for its eggs or for cod bait,
thousands burned alive for fuel to melt down others' fat.[2] Passen-
ger pigeons that once flew in hundred-mile-long streams over the
prairies, so thick they blotted out the sun, perhaps the most
abundant bird species ever to live on Earth,[3] no longer exist at all.
Buffalo numbered perhaps seventy million in North America
prior to Europeans' arrival on the prairies; they were reduced to
only a few hundred less than a century later. Some subspecies,
now extinct, were larger than elephants.[4] Pilot whales, giving
birth and giving suck in shallow coastal bays, were shot with
cannons or driven onto the beaches and left to die, then cut up,
often still alive, sometimes after two or three days of slowly
collapsing under their own weight waiting for the butchers to
finish their companions.[5] In the heyday of deep-sea whaling it
was no longer whales that were navigational hazards, but whale
carcasses.[6]

The destruction goes on. Vast tracts of rainforest, harboring
untold species that have not even been counted, are in flames at
this moment. Spotted owl, willow flycatcher, scarlet tanager,
lynx, bobcat, rhinoceros, elephant; all are or will be endangered.
Three dozen species have become extinct in the United States in
the past decade just waiting for Endangered Species Act designa-
tion.[7] Fully one quarter of the twenty thousand native plants in
America are threatened with extinction.[8] Blue whales, largest
living creatures on earth, have been reduced from 400,000–

500,000 in Antarctic waters alone to between six hundred and three thousand worldwide.[9] The use of whales and other cetaceans for target practice (machine gunning, depth charging, ramming) by the world's navies continues to be so common that NATO commanders are surprised when there are protests.[10] Fishermen and hunters worldwide still slaughter any inconvenient predator (wolf, dolphin, bobcat . . .) that (they think) threatens their catches. It is the hunter's article of faith, despite conclusive counterevidence, that killing predators creates more game for the hunt: as I write, Alaska is reopening the aerial wolf hunt for this purpose. Fossey's endangered mountain gorillas, hunted nearly to extinction, their hands sold abroad as ashtrays, are now tourist attractions, succumbing to human diseases and becoming such pawns of global entertainment industries and political power struggles that the gorilla featured in the Hollywood movie based on Fossey's life was assassinated by unknown assailants in the Rwandan civil war.[11] Even the chimps of Gombe are threatened: they may not survive in the wild.[12] Old-growth forest in Oregon and Washington, much of it on public land, may be entirely clear-cut in a generation. Almost as much land in the lower forty-eight states is covered by roads and parking lots as is designated wilderness. An area the size of Indiana is occupied just by lawns. The drinking water in Des Moines, Iowa, is so contaminated that nitrate levels are featured, along with the ubiquitous air pollution indices on the evening news. The groundwater on the Wisconsin prairie where I grew up, and close to Aldo Leopold's prairie farm, now contains so many nitrates (fertilizer leachate) that it kills babies. Even space is polluted: 3,300 *tons* of junk now orbit the Earth, at 20,000 or more miles an hour, forcing spacecraft to dodge, affecting launch schedules, colliding with other pieces of junk, and creating even more small pieces of lethal metal. At the highest altitudes, much of this debris will orbit for millions of years.[13]

Only a little less familiar are slower and more indirect processes of destruction. Many species, even those apparently well protected, are dying out slowly as their habitat is destroyed. Migratory songbirds such as the tanagers are threatened by loss of habitat at both ends (they winter in the rainforests) as well as by pesticides at this end. The young produced by the twenty-seven previously wild California condors captured and transferred to breeding programs in zoos in 1987 may or may not reacclimate to the wild, and all the causes of their original decline remain: loss of habitat, poison (lead shot in dead animals not recovered by hunters), high-energy power lines. Of an unknown number of subspecies of wolves in North America (Edward Goldman distinguished twenty-three in 1945), seven are extinct (like the fabulous pure white Newfoundland wolf, *Canis lupus beothucus*, named after Newfoundland's original human inhabitants, the Beothuk Indians, likewise extinct), and the rest, surviving after a fashion even under the pressure of unparalleled destruction and dislocation, seem to have interbred with each other and with dogs and coyotes to the point that only two or three subspecies remain.[14] Bats, who once flew in huge clouds from caves, have been killed by the millions by one person sealing an entrance or destroying their hearing with a bomb; yet bats are the pollinators for a wide variety of crucial species, especially in the places where their numbers have been most reduced.[15] Blue whales move in groups that may be too isolated to interbreed. Even with a global population in the thousands, the species may be dying out.[16] North Atlantic right whales, after not being hunted for fifty years, still number only about 150.[17]

Inconceivable pain, horror, and holocaust (literally, "casting whole into the fire"—think of the burning rainforests), lie behind these briefly listed facts. Loss to untold numbers of animals, to the future of the whole Earth, and to those humans who have lived close to those animals and to the land. Aboriginal people worldwide (fifty million tribal people still live in the rainforests, according to Gore's *Earth in the Balance*),[18] are being uprooted or killed off, by outright murder or starvation, dislocation, disease. Often the vanishing is quiet, hidden, and of no concern to the dominant civilization that moves in to fill the vacuum or just lets the ghost towns (ghost cultures, ghost languages, ghost possibilities) crumble into dust. Eskimo communities, visited once by a whaling ship, died to a person the next winter. Indian genocide through smallpox-infected blankets was a deliberate U.S. government policy; similar things go on today in the Amazon.[19] The extermination of the plains buffalo was a deliberate attack on the Plains Indians.[20] Often the natives are the only humans who can give a fully situated and *live* voice to the losses of the animals. A Nisqually Indian spokesperson, speaking of the salmon—*the* being who for all the Northwest Indians "gathers" the landscape—lamented their nearly complete extermination due to hydroelectric dams by saying that the Nisqually see salmon bleeding out of light bulbs.[21] We are the blind ones, seeing only the light.

People and noise are everywhere. Try walking Long Island's beaches today, seeking the bird voices as Whitman once did, or any kind of immersion in larger living worlds. Dune buggies, four-wheel-drive vehicles, the possessiveness of private landowners, and the sheer crush of beachgoers with their radios make any kind of reflectiveness or poetry-awakening ecstasy impossible. Birds cannot even nest on the shore. Motorboats, cars, lawn mowers drown out any songs; what Paul Shepard so evocatively describes as "the vast and articulate silence of the wild"—not "silent" at all, in truth, not always even quiet, but speaking *subtly*—is no more. Even in the wilderness you seldom can go very long without hearing engines: planes overhead, chain saws, cars in the valleys. Lawn mowers, leaf blowers, motorcycles, generators, snowblowers, snowmobiles, trains. The Environmental Protection Agency reports that eighty million Americans suffer significant disruption by noise; twenty million have suffered hearing loss.[22]

Sound alone may constitute cetaceans' expressive universe. Yet we subject them too to human noise—underwater drilling, boat motors of all sorts—without any thought of what the effects on them might be. A tenfold reduction in the distances they can communicate—from thousands to hundreds of miles—may be one major factor in blue whales' inability to interbreed.[23] If anything, the very fact that cetaceans and other marine animals make "noise" is used against them. Barry Lopez cites a Canadian government Environmental Impact Statement for an underwater drilling operation, a continuously noisy business: the racket, says this report, "would not be expected to be a hazard because of . . . the assumed high level of amibient underwater noise" already present.[24] Whale signaling, their entire expressive, communicative medium, is reduced to noise—all it *could* be to some oil-industry consultant in Toronto—and all noise is supposed to be the same. How could more hurt?

The omnipresence of artificial light in cities dissolves any real sense of darkness. Even the countryside is being turned into an extended, dimly lit suburbia: all the neighboring farms back in the Wisconsin contryside where I grew up, for instance, now have bright outdoor fluorescents. Here the "reduction" of the sense world is staggering; it is, as it were, immediately cut in half. *We don't know the dark.* We are never provoked by its eerie questions, at once turned inward and ever more acutely tuned outward, thrown onto the resources of the ears and nose. Animals who depend on the dark for cover or adaptation die or move (but where?). "Sea turtles, mistaking the glow of coastal communities for moonlight on water, head inland to be squashed on beachfront highways. Migrating birds slam into doom against the glittering confusion of office towers."[25] The owls leave.

Our own bodies too work on rhythms that may be impossible

to "tune" when we can't see moon or stars. Menstrual cycles mirror the moon and can still be coordinated by it—except that in all of our cities the moon is at best a dim background light. Women who want to regulate their cycles in this way are advised to shut their curtains and use a light. It is astonishing to remember that until the twentieth century most astronomers made their observations from townhouse windows in the centers of the great European cities. Today we must build telescopes in the most remote places and peaks, destroying more wild habitat in the process, or else launch them into space. Astronomers predict a nearly starless night, worldwide, by the late twenty-first century.[26] "It is a measure of the degree to which we have polluted our skies," writes physicist Chet Raymo, "that while almost everyone has heard of the Milky Way, surprisingly few people in the developed countries have seen it."

> I am thinking of an evening not long ago when I was far from city lights under a sky of crystalline clarity. The earth was tented with stars, stars so numerous they appeared as a continuous fabric of light. The Milky Way flowed like a luminous river from north to south, banked with dark shoals, eddied in glittering pools. . . . Such skies never fail to excite the imagination. Certain constellations—Orion or Ursa Major—are perhaps the oldest surviving inventions of the human mind. The depth and beauty of the night inspired religious and philosophical speculation. Science and mathematics had their origins in the questions posed by the night, by the lopsided circlings of sun and stars and the movements of the planets on their shuttlecock courses.[27]

Air pollution is reducing the acuity of daytime vision too. Visibility in the eastern United States has been reduced by *80 percent,* from ninety miles to fifteen, even in the countryside.[28]

Noise, light; then there is *speed.* Speed too rearranges and disconnects our senses, and dislocates and "reduces" other animals as well. Driving in a car, one loses touch with all of the land's smells and sounds, and most of its sights, not to mention one's own body. Walking is a drastically different experience. There may be a profound cultural loss as well. Gary Snyder, visiting Australia under the auspices of the Aboriginal Arts Board, drives across the desert in the back of a pickup with a Pintubi elder. Remember that even what appears almost a featureless wasteland to Europeans and Americans is in fact a richly varied and deeply historical landscape to the aboriginals, where every spot has its story, and one travels, both physically and mentally, by telling the stories, by singing the "songlines." "As we rolled along the dusty road," writes Snyder,

> [the elder] began speaking very rapidly to me. He was talking about a mountain over there, telling me a story about some wallabies that came to that mountain and got into some kind of mischief with some lizard girls. He had hardly finished that and he started in on another story about another hill over there and another story over there. I couldn't keep up. I realized after about half an hour of this that these were tales to be told while *walking*, and that I was experiencing a speeded-up version of what might be leisurely told over several days of foot travel.[29]

One imagines all sorts of depth and nuance lost, the stories tumbling over one another, finally unintelligible or at least skeletonized. And that is only at, say, thirty miles per hour. We might have some sort of approximation to the present state of things if we imagine traveling over the same landscape at *jet* speed. Nothing at all remains.

Speed remakes the very face of the world. Think of the nationwide homogeneity of the interstate highway system. Think of the look of American lawns. Michael Pollan argues that the function of the uniform lawn in suburbia is to create a kind of parkway, for the *motorist*.[30] Other animals must either adjust, move, or die. Road kills are one of the only ways that most Americans now encounter certain species of wild animals: raccoon, oppossum, skunk. "Road kill" becomes our very idea of those animals. Oppossums, naturally shy, nocturnal, the only marsupial in North America, padding along on feet whose imprints look almost exactly like human hands; but mangled roadside pile the next morning, pecked at by crows, virtually unidentifiable, is all we know.

All of this is familiar. All of us sometimes recognize some degree of "reduction" of larger living worlds, both subtle and not subtle at all, though perhaps its true extent is seldom recognized—Farley Mowat, in an almost unbearable passage concluding his *Sea of Slaughter*, contrasts the primeval world, absolutely packed with animal life, with the single silent seagull wheeling by his window today[31]—and perhaps it is no longer even recognizable, so far have we come. Aldo Leopold's career as a forester was more than half over before he realized that the lands he was trying to protect were already "sick"—his own word.[32] Until he traveled to some truly primeval Mexican desert lands, he had never seen healthy ecosystems at all. And that was half a century ago. Think about it: there may be nowhere left for a modern Leopold to have such an epiphany.

Sick land becomes, by default, our model of health. Radically reduced realities become our only realities. This process, perhaps just as much as our outright slashing and burning, is the destroyer of so much of the finest in our world; and it is this, I think, much more than our officially dismissive philosophies, that finally justifies us in dismissing the rest of the world as if it could not possibly be as interesting or as deep as the humanized world that is replacing it. At the same time, though, the self-fulfilling character of this dismissal is not easy to recognize. Its invisibility is part of its charm, so to speak. It is almost too close to us to be seen.

Wild animals have been mostly eradicated from our experience. One result is that we believe whatever we're told about them, however sentimental or hateful. This is, I suppose, the simplest kind of self-fulfilling belief: since no experience is possible that contradicts the belief, the belief is secure. Chickens are dumb, wolves are hateful, pigeons are automata; too often there is no way for us to learn better. The philosopher Thomas Hobbes, to whom we owe the alleged insight that life in nature is "nasty, poor, brutish, and short," was a city dweller in the midst of a civil war. He knew nothing at all about nature; he only projected the human savagery he saw around him onto it.

When more-than-human worlds are veiled from us, as for example by noise or light or speed, the result is *at least* ignorance. But it is usually more. The resident animals, like night predators in a light-polluted land, are killed or driven away, the cultures that know animal ways or have preserved an intimate knowledge of the history of the land are dislocated and destroyed, and so in the end the veil has nothing to cover. With the coming of Wisconsin corporate farms, down went the copses and windbreaks of my youth, on went the pesticides, and now the land itself is simplified and the songbirds (meadowlarks, whippoorwills) are gone, poisoned, or deprived of habitat. The older and more complex ecosystems are themselves gone, not merely veiled. A whole world is being reduced to what the new corporate-farm managers thought it was in the first place—and, again, it is reduced precisely *because* they held a reduced view of it in the first place. Eventually all of us will look at the land and have no idea it could be anything else.

The process turns more sinister as it turns more deliberate. Consider what is done to animals on "factory farms." They are reduced to the barest fragments of their potential selves. For one thing, confinement itself makes their natural development impossible. Chickens in cages cannot even spread their wings; calves meant for veal are not allowed to move or eat what they need for muscle development; sows are sometimes not even allowed the chance to stand up. Almost always, confinement also pushes animals past the point that their social instincts offer them any emotional and social equilibrium. When not raised in cages that give each bird a total space the size of a shoebox, cutting them off from any social relations whatsoever, chickens may be raised one hundred thousand to a giant shed, and have to be "debeaked" (their beaks cut off, sometimes several times in their short lives) so that they don't peck each other to death in their fury and confusion.[33] Moreover, breeding is used to help along this very process. All "stock" are bred for maximum weight gain. Pigs are often so bloated that they cannot even copulate without human help, and since, not surprisingly, this tends to spoil the sows' mood (yes pigs have moods), wholly artificial methods are coming into vogue.[34] There are already breeds of chicken who gain weight so fast that they cannot walk. Deformities and unexplained deaths abound. Research veterinarians argue that chickens now "might have been bred to grow so fast that they are on the verge of structural collapse"[35]—while genetic engineers speak with enthusiasm about soon breeding chickens that have no heads at all.[36] The final elimination of everything that is not convenient and not profitable: of any kind of genuine mental life, or genuine life at all, for that matter.

Right now, there are still chickens (with heads) and pigs and cows in the world. We can therefore continue to have our fantasies about chickens pecking contentedly in barnyards and such, when the reality is more like an assembly line. But when an inkling of the actual reality penetrates our awareness, the actual result is even worse for the animals. Then we think that the stupid, psychotic, slothful (or vicious or cancer-prone) animals that we have made are in fact what those animals are really like. The better we know the actual creatures—now that confinement, radical under- or over-stimulation, and breeding have done their work—the worse for us as well as them.

This particular kind of self-fulfillment I propose to label "self-validating reduction." The term may seem forbidding, but the process is subtle and needs an exact name. Self-validating reduction: the animals are reduced to the barest shadows of what they might be and once were, partly on account of our prejudices and needs in the first place. After all, they are "just animals," and besides we need them for food. Then we look at their present condition—the condition we have made, but a responsibility that at the moment we conveniently forget—and we can only say, "See? They really *are* stupid, dirty, pitiful." That reduction, once carried out, justifies itself. But then treating these animals like no more than raw materials for our needs comes to seem, after the fact, perfectly justified. And then they are made even more deformed and instrumentalized, even more underdeveloped; then even more drastic and complete kinds of exploitation become conceivable; and we end up precisely with headless chickens. The circle closes completely.

Prejudice is not easy to sustain in the face of everyday evidence to the contrary. Self-validating reduction is, in effect, prejudice that manages to remove the contrary evidence. Then the claim against the prejudice is reduced to a kind of speculation, even "sentimentality," romanticism. Headless chickens or dogs bred for viciousness are not going to be candidates for "animal rights"; for the same reason, even the insistently "reduced" chickens of the present aren't candidates for animal rights either. Anyone who thinks so looks like a mere sentimentalist.

The same self-validating logic can and does work in the case of humans. Sexism excluded women from most higher education until very recently in America, on the grounds that women do not have the requisite intelligence for it; but then of course women were *made* less intelligent—were "reduced"—precisely by being denied higher education in the first place (and of course also by being constantly demeaned when attempting anything intellectual, by being burdened with mind-deadening work, and so on). So the reduction validated itself; again, the circle closed. Similar things can be and have been said about racism. Frederick Douglass, campaigning against slavery in 1854, wrote:

> Ignorance and depravity, and the inability to arise from degradation to civilization and respectability, are the most usual allegations against the oppressed. The evils most fostered by slavery and oppression are precisely those which slaveholders and oppressors would transfer from their system to the inherent character of their victims. Thus the very crimes of slavery become slavery's best defense. By making the enslaved a character fit only for slavery, they excuse themselves for failing to make the slave a freeman.[37]

Self-reinforcing effects may be deliberately planned for. Bruno Bettleheim argues that the Nazi concentration camps were designed to *make* the inmates subhuman, thus confirming the Nazis' prejudices and making systematic murder (as well as the continued dehumanization of the inmates) possible.[38]

With respect to other humans, though, there is at least a countervailing respect for human dignity—however poorly it is sometimes expressed!—that serves as a kind of protection against the worse excesses of self-validating reduction. Moreover, by demanding that other humans be treated with a certain respect, it actually helps to create the conditions under which human autonomy and creativity begin to show themselves, and so people begin to *invite*, even demand, respect. Self-validating logic, in short, goes both ways: we are confirmed in including those we include, just as we are confirmed in excluding those we exclude. We could speak as well of "self-validating inclusion" or "self-fulfilling respect." But the point again is that there is, at present, much less to resist the self-validating reduction of other animals, little that begins to make a space within which *their* autonomy and creativity might begin to emerge. The result is that it does not. Instead, it is systematically suppressed, closed out.

The same logic works in very subtle ways and pervades the world. Ethological research aims to approach other animals in their own terms, and even some philosophers are not unwilling to be shown that "animals can think" or that, as one dolphin researcher put it, "there's somebody in there." The problem is that this posture, too, full of goodwill or at least open-mindedness as it thinks itself to be, often remains profoundly inept, in the wrong key, refusing precisely the trust and identification that might make a genuine relation to other creatures possible. The demand that others "prove" themselves, for example, is not a demand we make of each other; such a demand already represents a way of closing ourselves off from the creature in question (and that's just it: "in question"). Moreover, it is not simply a matter of "veiling" the other creatures. Making such a demand affects them in turn: it "reduces" them in *fact*. Human beings trip over their own feet when treated with such distance and skepticism, and there is no reason to expect other animals to do better, especially when they are exquisitely more sensitive to the affective environment than we are. Not to mention that "in there" is precisely what fully sensed creatures are *not*; we are "out here," moving in a rich and responsive shared world. To look so insistently "in there" is already to guarantee that what you find will be very strange, and reduced. If you find anything at all.

So other animals are "reduced" to objects, even if just objects for research. Visiting a research station in the rainforest at which howler monkeys are being studied, Jim Nollman is assured that the monkeys are fundamentally unsociable, retreating to the forest canopy whenever humans are around. So they have behaved. This looks like—in fact, *is*—an objective description. On further inquiry, Nollman learns that the zoologists study the monkeys by attaching radio transmitters to their necks. To attach the transmitters they have to tranquilize the monkeys. To tranquilize the monkeys they shoot them with tranquilizer guns, dropping them out of the canopy a hundred or more feet to the forest floor. The zoologists consider this technique unproblematic, "objective," purely scientific; and they clearly regard Nollman, a musician who tries to use music to create a shared space between humans and animals, as a sentimental and unscientific meddler.[39] Surely, though, what looks like a genuine discovery about the monkeys' sociability is more likely a distortion imposed on them by the profoundly, almost unbelievably antisocial strategy of the researchers. Any creature with a modicum of intelligence would stay away from them. The scientists' "objectivity" succeeds only in *reducing* the monkeys to objects, blocking any genuine connection at all.

One could say that this study was just badly designed. But nearly all animal research shares its operating principles. Nearly all animal researchers have been taught, as a very condition of being objective, to eradicate even the most obscure impulses of identification with other animals. So it never occurs to them to ask how they themselves would feel being shot out of trees like the monkeys; or how they would react if, like two elephants in a UCLA study, they were given virtually lethal dosages of LSD daily for two months.[40] Consequently, more generally, it never occurs to the scientists that they themselves might be sociable with the test animals, and as a result they are left no way to open up a space within which the animals might respond sociably to them.

This is, of course, bad enough. The animals are thoroughly "reduced" before any recognition can even be attempted. They are emphatically *not* approached as cohabitants of the world, as in any sense kin. The poor scientist giving LSD to elephants could only regard their behavior as "inappropriate" when they repeatedly charged him. But still worse is this: precisely as a consequence, the animals are pushed away. Because the scientists cannot envision the monkeys as cohabitants of the world, the monkeys are *driven out* of cohabitation. The only socially sensitive behavior left to them is to act socially insensitive or, like the elephants, to charge—which of course the scientists misinterpret.

And these are cases where one supposes that the intentions are reasonably good. The most common cases lie in between good intentions and outright reconstruction: cases perhaps of indifference. The effects, the reduction, may be subtle from a human point of view, but devastating to the animals. As Mary Midgley remarks, "any spontaneous, enterprising behavior on the part of an ox, dog, or horse tends to strike its owner as wasteful, stupid, or obstreperous, not as evidence that it has a mind of its own. He views the animal mainly in its functional light simply as a thing."[41] Thoreau writes somewhere of coming upon a herd of cows running about, like huge rats or kittens or deer; then he reflects that "a sudden loud *Whoa!* would have dampened their ardor at once, reducing them from venison to beef." Beef they must be. These days an animal showing sportiveness or spontaneity or enterprise is even more thoroughly *made* into a thing: more tightly leashed, returned to harsher training to remove any latent spontaneity, or abandoned or killed, thus literally reduced to a thing. "Beef cattle," we call them; we even name them for the food we make of them. There is no tolerance for any creatureliness emerging in the "production factors." The most intensively used animals no longer even get old enough. Chickens live about seven years naturally; the typical battery broiler lives seven weeks.[42]

Wild animals are also reduced in ultimately self-validating ways. Animals that originally were indifferent or even friendly to humans were *made* hostile and "aggressive." Habitat destruction pushes wolves and bears into competition with humans; hunting creates fear and anger. Even polar bears coexisted easily with aboriginal peoples and were not hostile to the first whites in the Arctic.[43] Now, stereotypically, they attack—and the stereotype at least sometimes is true. You or I, pushed as they have been into desperation, would do the same thing. The surviving Florida manatees, placid channel-dwelling "sea cows," cousins to the elephants, are so scarred by powerboat propellers that researchers now use their scar patterns to identify them.[44] Their very identities are defined in terms of the mutilations humans have imposed on them.

Meanwhile, it is only one more form of dismissal for us to imagine that wild animal populations do not themselves evolve, and may therefore be changed in the direction of less complex or intelligent behaviors by our very lack of responsiveness (or systematic misconstruction of their responses), rather like human populations that rapidly lose their cultural distinctiveness after contact with a dominant civilization that may (*may*) not be ill intentioned but simply has no place for or interest in them. It is a measure of how little credit we give other animals that the very idea of animal social evolution within the space of single lifetimes surprises us. Certainly it would have staggering implications for wildlife biology. Yet there are clear examples. Whole pods of California gray whales learned from a single whale to like human petting; it now seems to be part of the whales' culture (this the very species that whalers called the "devilfish" because it had the gall to try to kill humans who were trying to kill it).[45] The U.S. Navy allegedly tried to train dolphins—who, remember, played with Greek children in antiquity and our own children now, whose goodwill toward humans is legendary—to kill enemy divers and swimmers. Did anyone pause to think what would have happened had such behaviors caught on among the highly social dolphins? Barry Lopez cites Nunamiut hunters speculating about the evolution of new behaviors among wolves, and concludes: "If social animals evolve, then what you learn today may not apply tomorrow. . . . In striving to create a generalized static animal you have lost the real, dynamic animal."[46] Likewise, if the general effect of other animals' increasingly unavoidable contact with humans is a degeneration, a *de*volution, then this "loss" may not simply be what I called above a "veiling" but a genuine loss by the animal of probably irrecoverable possibilities.

We come, finally, to the land itself. Self-validating reduction works just as emphatically here.

For Native Americans, the land was a living being. Aldo Leopold invites us to see it as a moral community of which we are "plain biotic citizen." Both notions are opposed to the commercial view of land as essentially a subdividable and consumable commodity. Yet the commercial view is hardly just a "view." In most places it is *true:* that is, it has become a self-validating view because the land has in fact been divided and consumed in accord with it. And I mean that it is "true" quite literally, just as it may have been true quite literally that women were less fit for higher education than men in the nineteenth century. It is not just that the land *seems* dead. It *is* dead, for example, when a parking lot replaces a woodland. Or it is radically degraded, as when a "monoculturing" farm (growing just one crop, killing everything else with herbicides and pesticides) replaces the old mixed-community farms in which weeds were tolerated and insect pests kept within ecological limits (and fed on the weeds). Or when it is laid out, mile after square mile, in an unvarying grid pattern, nearly all vegetation gone except at the edges of roads, the rest plowed under and planted in the same crop. Just fly over Nebraska. The self-validating view: the land is boring, simple, homogenous, "all the same"—so we have *made* it.

As a group exercise I sometimes have my students read through a newspaper, paying attention to the ways in which the nonhuman world is represented. In the advertisements, "nature" turns out to mean expensive vacations halfway around the world (no "nature" of any interest is ever *next* to us; it has to cost money to get there). In the news, nature is an object of manipulation, exploitation, and maybe (still usually somewhere else, so as not to endanger anyone's property rights) a matter of concern. One of the most striking but also least-noticed representations of nature is in the real estate listings. The message: land is something for possession, and comes in "pieces." That message is so familiar that students actually need help seeing it. Yet the very idea of a "piece" of land helps to break down its wholeness, making it instead a series of checkers or counters in economic transactions, suggesting that what happens in one place is not essentially related to what happens anywhere else, on someone else's "piece." And consequently the land *is* broken into pieces; hence it *becomes* no more than "pieces." The economic view becomes self-validating.

I have mentioned the "veiling" effects of speed, noise, and light on other animals. The land itself is also reduced. The demand for progressively faster speeds, for example, produces a demand for progressively more massive rearrangement of the land to suit the needs of automobiles. Little one-lane, hedgerow-lined roads, like those of the English countryside, often worn well below the surface and consequently nearly invisible and inaudible until you practically fall into them, are replaced by larger and larger roads until we have six-lane superhighways whose noise and visual presence dominate whole valleys. Along the Connecticut secondary roads I used to drive, "developers" are taking bulldozers to whole hillsides, rearranging them to suit someone's idea of what a hillside should look like, or to suit the structural needs of the enormous houses that follow. The ancient face of the land is gone, and the land truly becomes no more than raw material for rearrangement into patterns that suit our convenience or passing tastes.

The land has suffered a long time. One version of the Ten Commandments itself contains the commands that the Israelites "tear down the [pagan] altars, break their images, cut down the groves"[47] ("For the Lord Your God, whose name is Jealous, is a jealous God"). Sacredness does not dwell in this world—God is separate, the real life of the spirit is elsewhere—and therefore, precisely in order to make this radically new and separate sense of sacredness plausible, the sacred spots in this world had to be destroyed. God knew what He was doing. *Cut down their sacred groves*: destroy the places of power of the ancient world, eliminate those places next to us, among us, that speak of the sacred, that hold the numinous here. Christians did the same thing well into medieval times.[48] Paul Shepard calls it "the evangelical desacralizing of place." Then spirit must flee this world, and the transcendent realm remains the only place it can go. The original denial of sacredness to this world becomes self-fulfilling.

Christianity's world-devaluation itself arose in a region that had already in many ways been "reduced." Long before the birth of Jesus, the great juniper forests of Persia were gone; the cedars of Lebanon were going; the Tigris and Euphrates Rivers, irrigating the "cradles of civilization," were carrying massive silt loads; the hills of the entire Mediterranean region were stripped and eroded. Odysseus got his scar from a boar that surprised him while hunting on Mount Parnassus: the woods were so thick that he got too close. By the Golden Age, Parnassus was, as it is is now, nothing but rock. The Greeks needed wood to build ships for their wars, the soil washed into the sea, and now you can see for miles. Not that any boars remain to worry about. In short, again, by the time of Jesus the reduction of the land was already an accomplished fact. The world—the actual physical world, the health of the land—already was "in decline." Christianity both expressed that sense of decline and contributed to it, speeding up its tempo and eventually exporting it to ecologically richer and more innocent places.

There remains, in actual fact, less and less about the land to compel us. We can barely imagine how enormously different the world of even a few centuries ago actually was. Mostly we can only characterize it in negatives: not pervaded by noise, no jet trails in the sunsets. Owls and moose and the great ancient trees still around us, still in our dreams. Then think of the ancient world, with its sacred groves, all-pervading quiet, the panorama of the heavens opening up every night unimpeded by light and air pollution everywhere; wildness still at the very margins of the city. In the city. The blossoms of the yew tree under which one might fall asleep on a medieval afternoon were mild hallucinogens: a catnap could turn into a trip to the Venus Mountain.[49] But now the yews are almost gone too, and the Venusberg is the stuff only of opera. We must visit the zoo or the opera to regain even the faintest sense of what was once ordinary human experience, probably misunderstanding it the while as "supernatural."

We come, finally, to the most modern form of world-reduction: what the French philosopher Jean Baudrillard and other critics call "simulation."[50] This is at once both the subtlest and the most pervasive form of destruction: seemingly as far as possible from outright destruction and yet at least as threatening, even when not actually collaborating with the outright destroyers only slightly behind the scenes.

I have said that we are increasingly confined to more and more urbanized and humanized environments. But there appear to be opposite trends too. More and more people are visiting national parks, for example, so much so that the crush of people is itself a serious problem. But at least we seek out and experience nature this way? In fact, there is nothing so pure or unproblematic here. Going to the parks is an expression of a deeply automotive culture, just as the initial formation of many of the parks was strongly supported and shaped by the railroads (Yellowstone owes its existence to the Northern and Union Pacific Railroads, among others).[51] Car culture is pervasive. Roads go everywhere, and most visitors never leave their cars except to eat, sleep, and go to the john: "In Grand Teton National Park, 93% of the visitors never visit the backcountry. If visitors do make other stops, it is at designated picturesque "scenes" or educational exhibits presenting interesting facts—the names of peaks, a bit of history—or, very occasionally, for passive recreation, a ride in a boat or an organized nature walk."[52] So we have experienced the park, we know what "the wild" and "nature" really are? Albert Borgmann, writing of what he calls "the widespread and easy acceptance of equivalence between commodities and things even when the experiential differences are palpable," goes on:

> People who have traveled through Glacier Park in an air-conditioned motor home, listening to soft background music and having a cup of coffee, would probably answer affirmatively when asked if they knew the park, had been in the park, or had been through the park. Such people have not felt the wind of the mountains, have not smelled the pines, have not heard the red-tailed hawk, have not sensed the slopes in their legs and lungs, have not experienced the cycle of day and night in the wilderness.[53]

They do *not* know the park. From the point of view of the senses, the experience could not be more radically different. Of the motor-home visit, Borgmann concludes: "the experience has not been richer than one gained from a well-made film viewed in suburban Chicago." In fact, *all* of the senses are required, and time, and an openness to the unexpected, and risk, and strain. (Of course, of course, for some people it may be that only a motor-home visit is physically possible. But let us not suppose that what one then experiences is "nature.")

Put on the pack and go into the woods. But Jack Turner reports from the wild:

We see signs and hike horse trails and cross sturdy bridges and find maps on large boards at trail junctions. We meet patrolling rangers, Scout groups working on character, and the National Outdoor Leadership School teaching "wilderness" skills in a corporate management seminar. We meet trail crews, pack trains, and hikers galore. . . . We camp by a lake, the outlet of which is filled with spawning golden trout. We notice they are thin as smelt. They are not indigenous to these mountains. Around camp, many small trees have been cut down by Basque sheepherders. The trails of their herds are ubiquitous; domestic sheep still graze this wilderness. In autumn we find hunting camps the size of military installations, the hunters being better armed than Green Berets. Many of the camps use salt licks to lure the deer, elk, and moose. If we wander out of this narrow "wilderness zone," we walk straight into clear-cut forest, logging roads, and oil wells.[54]

Mining is allowed, even in the wilderness, under the "multiple use" provision of the 1964 Wilderness Act—as are water prospecting, water-conservation works, power projects, transmission lines, and roads.[55] Turner concludes: "This is no longer a wild, no longer a wilderness. . . . We *believe* we make contact with the wild, but this is an illusion. In both the national parks and wilderness areas we accept a reduced category of experience, a semblance of wild nature, a fake. And no one complains." Well, of course. We have no sense—and, increasingly, *can* have no sense—that things could be any different. Any such hint smacks immediately of sentimentality and nostalgia, as with our sense that other animals could be anything other than mindless battery chickens or the bored, apathetic animals that we see (feeling the same way ourselves for the most part) in zoos. ("Simulation" again: we take our children to the zoos "to see the wild animals"—like ocean-spanning whales confined to single concrete tanks. And fed discretely: it's against the law to feed live animals to other animals in public.)[56]

We cheerfully substitute commodities in place of real experience everywhere. Nothing is sacred, not even the sacred. Egypt is planning a hotel and casino on top of Mount Sinai, including a lighted walkway to the spot where Moses met God.[57] So now we will be able to "experience" the site of one of humankind's most profound religious experiences, then stroll back to the Marriott for an evening of blackjack and maybe shrimp scampi. The Greek Orthodox monastery at the foot of Sinai, cradling the skulls of fourteen centuries of its dead monks in its charnel house and sheltering what tradition says was the Burning Bush, an olive tree that has been putting out fresh green shoots for three thousand years, will be overrun and destroyed. Or perhaps the Egyptian government could hire people to impersonate the monks, like in Williamsburg? A plastic olive tree would take less tending. The point is that we would not know the difference. Yet another numinous spot (one of the few that even Christianity at least officially respects) will be gone.

"In other parts of Africa," the author Paul Bowles remarked, "you are aware of the earth beneath your feet, of the vegetation and the animals; all power seems concentrated in the earth. In North Africa the earth becomes the less important part of the landscape because you find yourself constantly raising your eyes to look at the sky. . . ." Is that the reason the three great monotheisms were born in the desert . . . ?

The Lord "descended upon [Mount Sinai] in fire," *Exodus* records. The Lord gave the Law to Moses there: "And all the people saw the thunderings, and the lightnings, and the noise of the trumpet, and the mountain smoking. . . ." Today a visitor sees the massive granite front of Horeb that rises perpendicularly out of moonscape and in the autumn and winter months may be surrounded by sudden clouds, thunder, lightning, and lashing rains.[58]

It is precisely that wildness to which all the Marriotts of the world are opposed; that wildness of God Himself that even His own (self-appointed) spokespeople rush to tame. Remember that when that God of Sinai finally responds to Job's complaints, he does not offer some kind of tedious moral justification; instead he merely lifts the curtain on what Thoreau, many centuries later, called "that vast, savage, howling mother of ours, Nature, lying all around, and with such beauty." It is another one of those astonishing points in the Bible where all creation erupts. Ibis swoop through; lions and mountain goats come darting from their lairs; hail, thunder, lightning again. This is a *wild God:*

> Who laid the cornerstones of the earth
>   when all the stars of the morning were singing with joy . . . ?
> Who pent up the sea behind closed doors
>   when it lept tumultuous out of the womb,
> When I wrapped it in a robe of mist
>   and made black clouds its swaddling bands . . . ?[59]

But all of this, like nature itself, has too raw an edge for us now. Someone might get hurt. Why don't we just rent the video?

Television, of course, is the prime form and worst perpetrator of simulation. Television is now so pervasive that it is apparently no longer possible for psychologists to find a group of nonwatchers large and representative enough to test. (They can test only high and low users. So if television as *such* rots the mind, psychology will never be able to prove it.) Well-intentioned friends have seriously argued that they really do learn something about animals from watching television specials about endangered predators, about nature from watching "Wild Kingdom" and its modern equivalents (rock stars embracing the latest fad species on MTV?). I find this unbelievable. The medium is irredeemable. Look at the total message: what actually is learned about "nature" from low-resolution pictures of animal or scenery projected into your living room between beer and auto commercials, programmed in convenient segments among a dozen other segments, "the News," the soaps? (Nature as one "channel" among others? "What's on tonight, honey?" Whatever "nature" is, according to television, it is *not* whatever is outside of your image-filled living room right now.) *Nothing* of the tempo or the grain or the complexity of actual living worlds remains. What one "learns" is a falsehood of the deepest kind. It would be better not to try to show "nature" at all. Even the "message," taken in the narrowest possible sense, is radically distorted. Just one example:

> By taking the waiting out of watching, wildlife films make creatures appear less modest and retiring than they really are. Animals become almost promiscuously available on television. We get lingering close-ups. The animals are fully revealed. There are no empty landscapes. That . . . is why visitors to our national parks expect wildlife to be accessible. Says National Park Service naturalist Glen Kaye, "Whatever the hour of the day, the question is 'What meadow do I see the deer or the elk or the bear, *right now?*' There is no sense that the animals might not be available."[60]

The point is not just that people like this annoy the rangers. Again remembering the plasticity of the senses, one fears that the effects of our immersion in television's "right now" world will be that any kind of waiting, any sense that there are rhythms in this world that are much different than television's, will be lost. We will take the world to *be* what television shows us, and have no patience for any other. And then any other will be all the more readily lost.

Almost everything is infected. The wild and free are reduced to the terms of cars and military hardware ("A falcon is built for speed. Powerful but streamlined, a falcon can streak across the sky like a jet fighter, drop like a dive-bomber, turn on a dime" —this is from *Audubon* magazine).[61] No one finds it odd that

Florida's last and endangered panthers are fitted with green reflective collars to keep them from getting hit on the roads;[62] the idea that automotive culture could have any limits is apparently less imaginable than that the panther should, one way or another, be sacrificed to it. The trivialization of names is now universal: the ubiquitous "Deer Run," "Hidden Pond," and the like for condominium developments where no self-respecting deer will ever be seen and where the ponds are artificial and definitely not hidden. This is what we are now offered as "nature."

To try to live in any world besides the reduced and simulated world is now a constant struggle, where the victories are small, personal, and partial. The truth is that the only *whole* world we are at present offered is the wholly humanized world that offers us at best simulations of larger living worlds. By "whole" I mean: one can live in this world without ever coming out of it, because one lives in it not alone but in concert with most of one's fellows and all of society's major institutions. Everything supports and reinforces it: you literally have to climb the walls to get out, and even then you hear the noise. On every American Airlines flight, right after takeoff, a flight attendant comes over the intercom trying to entice people to join the airline's Frequent Flyer club, enumerating all the ways one can add miles: by making long-distance phone calls, staying in certain hotels, making certain stock transactions, car rentals, credit-card purchases. I watch the hills and trees flowing by beneath. What strikes me with almost overwhelming force at these times is that for people who live in what we might call the "credit-card world," these hills and trees in a sense don't really exist, or they exist only at the margins or as a form of obstacle to get around or over. At best, the natural world exists only in other places, as a kind of vacation land (as any number of states' license plates actually advertise) and exists in one's own place only as a kind of decoration, or nuisance. And for just these reasons the nature that really does exist is progressively being destroyed. The credit-card world is also the world of superhighways, airports, global networks of raw material extraction and manufacturing that are transforming and ruining the planet. Seeing only the commodities, reducing the world to certain goods and services, allows everything else, falling into darkness, to be treated as mere resource for commodity production. It is this that sends not explorers or poets into the wilderness but oil exploration crews. So far from being a mere reduction in our experience that leaves the world alone, the credit-card world is the very condition of blindness—the practical backdrop, so to speak—that allows the world as a whole to be transformed into more of what credit cards buy. We are rapidly losing any sense of what we are missing. The circle is closing.

6

Coming to Our Senses

I had just moved to a Long Island suburb when Hurricane Gloria struck in 1985. For the storm itself, people retreated to their basements. Then there was a day or so of removing fallen trees from the roads and being grateful that nothing worse had happened. But the electricity was out, and all signs were that it would stay out for a good long time. Food was spoiling in everyone's freezers. A few of the neighbors could still use their propane-powered outdoor grills. The result was that for nearly a week there were nightly barbecues for everyone in the neighborhood. People you usually saw only as they sped off to work would suddenly invite you over for lobster or steak, all you could eat. An entire lost civility and sense of community began to arise. Even more striking was the new scene in what had previously been a well-lighted and self-preoccupied neighborhood. Without electricity and with nowhere else to go, people would just sit for hours in someone's backyard and watch the full moon rise. It was the equinox moon, too: full and shimmering, massive and brooding in the absence of any other light, the likes of which few people had ever seen. For a week we lived on lobster and moonlight.

Finally the electricity came back on and people hurried back to their jobs and their televisions. Still, for a moment, we knew something else, another possibility, brooded over by the old moon. The winds reached out, touched a few power lines, and blew away the mass culture, and even the most jaded of suburbanites remembered the Earth. The sighs that greeted the return of what has become the modern world's "normality" were not for everyone sighs of relief but also, for some—for more of us perhaps than would admit it—were sighs of resignation, as the old routines returned. To resist them in normal times and in the typical places seems impossible. Instead we just once again shoulder the old burdens. Even so, though, some inkling remains that not everyone has lived or lives this way, that even now, even in the very midst of desolation, there are other possibilities.

It is only when we demand some kind of single, one-step, top-down "solution" to environmental crisis that we have no idea how to proceed. When the demand is for a range of *beginnings*—of gradual reopenings, new ways to live, launching out in a dozen directions, even in the midst of desolation—it is hardly even a puzzle what we should do. One immediate and simple beginning, one totally obvious possibility, is to try to live more often, more normally, the way Long Island lived temporarily for the week after Gloria: to live closer to the moon and the quiet.

Suppose that certain places were set aside as *quiet zones:* places where automobile engines and lawn mowers and airplanes were not allowed. People would live in such places; we would just leave our power tools and stereos and automobiles somewhere else. The aim would be modest, too: simply to make it possible to hear the birds and the winds and the silence once again. To literally "come back to our senses." If bright outside lights were also disallowed, one could see the stars at night, see the moons wax and wane, and feel the slow pulsations of the light over the seasons. The heaviness of the night could return. There *is* such a thing as real darkness, "darkness so thick you can cut it with a knife," only now we have forgotten what it is like. The stars could return, and the night creatures now exiled by the light.

This is not a utopian proposal. Unplug a few outdoor lights, reroute some roads, and in some places of the country we have a first approximation, even when the electricity is on. I live now in a not particularly unusual neighborhood well within the city limits of Raleigh, capital city of North Carolina, yet this very Saturday night my daughter went to sleep in my arms as we sat out on our porch and listened to the crickets and an owl in the dark. Only an occasional car intervened. What it would take to preserve and extend such spaces, in many regions and corners, is not necessarily so great. Return more neighborhood roads to local traffic only. Preserve owl habitat, plant wildflowers. Instead of more and more tract developments consuming cornfields and woodlots, let us try some experiments in creative zoning, make space for increasingly divergent styles of living on and with the land: experiments in recycling and energy self-sufficiency, for example; mixed communities of humans and other species; or other possibilities not yet even imagined. Canadian ecophilosopher Alan Drengson proposes the creation of "ecosteries"— "centers, facilities, stewarded land, Nature sanctuaries, where ecosophy [ecological philosophy] is learned, taught, and practiced"—on analogy to the medieval monasteries: "places where spiritual discipline and practice are the central purpose."[1] There is no reason that we must condemn ourselves to another ten thousand suburbs all the same. Almost all the alternatives would be *less* intrusive, less costly for municipalities to maintain, more interesting; the neighbors could hardly complain.

I do not mean that such places are for *everyone*. The point is to create a variety of places for something else, not to force everyone into one such type of place. Different quiet zones will no doubt have widely varied characters: everything from eco-monasteries to alternative suburbs are possible. This very experimentalism and modesty are in fact crucial. Making any particular "alternative" zone work requires a slow, concrete reconstruction of a way of life, a kind of sustained experiment. It also requires fine-grained and sustained attention to the character or spirit of the place—and places vary.

The point is also not that such a life would somehow just be "nice." It may sound like nothing so much as summer vacation. But that in itself is revealing. It is precisely the association of the more-than-human with the unimportant and marginal in our lives that has proved so desolating. Living in a quiet zone would be nothing like an "escape" for the all-too-familiar vacation weekend that in fact leaves everything we want to "escape" intact, just making it momentarily more bearable. Instead, it is to move the more-than-human permanently back to center stage: to re-*center*, not to "get away" at all. The aim in such quiet zones is not to exclude or even to marginalize humans, but instead to contextualize us, in our "everyday" lives, surrounding us with a more-than-human sense world. It is precisely *not* "vacation," in the sense that we "vacate" our usual lives and empty our time, but instead is a kind of *filling*. Not an escape but a return: a return, quite literally, to our senses.

Every example in this book has been an example of experience in such places: in the "mixed communities" that are still and already present in at least some of our homes or farms; in Goodall's and Fossey's jungle camps and Lorenz's Austrian village eaves; in *Song of Solomon*'s rendering of a whole people's love of their trees and farms and animals in their place, to them a holy land. In the "Earth Alive" with the insects of a summer evening. Thoreau writes from the top of Katahdin:

We walked over it with a certain awe. . . . It was a specimen of what God saw fit to make this world. . . . I stand in awe of my body, this matter to which I am bound has become strange to me. I fear not spirits, ghosts, of which I am one . . . but I fear bodies, I tremble to meet them. What is this Titan that has possession of me? Talk of mysteries! Think of our life in nature—daily to be shown matter, to come into contact with it—rocks, trees, wind on our cheeks! the *solid* earth! the *actual* world! the *common sense! Contact! Contact!*[2]

Katahdin is now a kind of icon for the backpackers of America, the northern terminus of the Appalachian Trail. But Thoreau's point is ultimately not about mountaintops at all. It is not about the icons of the wild. The "contact" he speaks of is the most *daily.* The "mysteries" lie *next* to us. That is what is awesome: "daily to be shown matter, to come into contact with it—rocks, trees, wind on our cheeks!" The examples are prosaic. The point is simple, simple, simple: if we are to have any sense of the natural rhythms of the light and any sense of the moving world of birds and winds, we must live in places where we can see the rhythms of the light and hear the sounds of the more-than-human world.

Quiet zones are only one possibility. In the midst of the worst city we can still imagine little "pocket parks," strategically placed, insulated from noise. "Quiet backs" are common in the older cities of Europe—small "green" areas, behind houses or public buildings, densely planted, perhaps connected by small footpaths and waterways—like the walk through the cathedral close in Chichester cited by Christopher Alexander and his colleagues in their synoptic tract *A Pattern Language,* where, "less than a block from the major crossroads of the town, you can hear the bees buzzing."[3] This is not only in the city but in the very middle of the busiest part of the city. The remergence of the more-than-human even in the city is not at all impossible, but we must *plan* for it.

Alexander and his colleagues make a variety of proposals to this effect, all of them offered as part of their general accounting of "the timeless way of building:" those "patterns," as they call them, often ancient though not necessarily even fully deliberate, that define the most livable and fulfilling of our cities, neighborhoods, and houses. Alexander and his colleagues propose interlocking "city–country fingers" that bring the open countryside within a short walk or bicycle ride from downtown. They calculate the maxiumum distance from home that a pocket park can lie and still attract walkers (two to three blocks). They calculate the optimum size for such parks. They uncover the patterns that underlie the attraction even of small but "enchanted" natural places, again in the very midst of the city: "layered" (gradual, phased) access, the presence of running and still water, the presence of animals (birds, snakes, goats, rabbits, wild cats). They plead for "site repair," for building on the worst parts of a piece of land rather than the best, so as to repair and improve the poorer parts while preserving the most precious, beautiful, and healthy parts (and honoring the fact that these parts are often slowly evolved and complex, not something that can be re-created elsewhere even if we or the "landscape contractor" try). They argue for the necessity of what they call "positive outdoor space": places partly enclosed by buildings and natural features so as to have a shape of their own, courtyards or partial courtyards, for example, as opposed to the shapeless outdoor space so familiar around the squarish and irregularly placed buildings of our suburbs and cities, and for "half-hidden gardens:" neither the entirely decorative traditional American front yard nor the wholly private back gardens of Europe, but an intermediate kind of space.[4]

Alexander's "quiet backs," and half-enclosed and transitional outdoor spaces, are similar to the places Wendell Berry calls "margins:" places, as he puts it, where domesticity and wildness meet, places like hedgerows, wood edges, desert oases, shorelines.[5] "Edge" is a related ecological term for the same thing. Access to water is also a fundamental "pattern" for Alexander, and shorelines are "margins" as well as, literally *and* ecologically, "edges":

> As a rule, the natural edges between water and shore are marked by a slow, rough transition. There is a certain well-marked sequence of changes in materials, texture, and ecology as one passes

from land to water. The human consequences of this transition are important: it means that people can walk lazily along the edge, without concern for their safety; they can sit at the edge and have their feet in the water. . . . Children can play in the water safely when the edge is gradual. . . . It has even been shown that children teach themselves to swim when they are free to play around a pool with an extremely gradual slope toward the deep.[6]

Again the message is that a regular but profound kind of "contact" with the more-than-human is possible, even easy; even, in fact, centuries old, already, in the older cities of the world. It takes only some sustained attentiveness to the simplest features of the design of urban places. The most impressive feature of Alexander's work is this sheer mindfulness about what we usually take for granted, and of simple hidden possibilities in the very midst of the familiar urban desolation. The city is not lost at all.

Then there is the matter of the house. Psychologically and historically, modern American houses all too often function as fortresses against the supposed dangers, human and nonhuman, of the "outside" world. It becomes hard for us to imagine anything else. Yet here too there are alternatives, in fact entire alternative traditions, even in America. Frank Lloyd Wright used the wall, freed from its support functions, as a delicate and deliberately ambiguous transition point between outside and in. Traditional (pre-airconditioning) southern houses half buried the first floor for coolness and used breezeways to amplify the faintest breeze—the winds were invited in. Native American styles still dominate parts of the Southwest, like adobe, made from the very clay of the building site, periodically replastered with the same: the buildings literally grow out of the earth. Other Native styles make it as clear as possible that people lived in larger communities. A tipi keeps nothing out by the wind; it is the *respect* of others that protects those within.

Once again we may turn to the work of Alexander and his colleagues for a set of "patterns" or guidelines for a way of building, this time building houses, that opens us to more-than-human worlds, and those worlds to us. Doors and windows, for starters, need to be rethought, done more deliberately. Rooms with windows or doors on more than one side make the outside more than one-dimensional, give it some sense of depth, make it a surrounding rather than a picture. Especially the south face of a building should open to the outdoors, and the most important rooms should lie along the south edge, both to fill the house with light and to tempt us outside in the most inviting direction.[7] Another crucial requirement for staying "in contact" is that a house and its grounds offer "ways of being partly inside, yet still connected to the outside:" some sense of permeability, interchange, intermediate realms is necessary. So

> [surround] the building . . . , along at least a part of its perimeter, by terraces, paths, steps, gravel, and earthen surfaces, which bring the floors outside, into the land. These surfaces are made of intermediate materials more natural than the floors inside the house—and more manmade than earth and clay and grass. The surface is part of the earth—and yet a little smoother, a little more beaten, more swept. . . . Brick terraces, tiles, and beaten earth tied into the foundations of the house all help make this connection.[8]

Remember, too, that the edges of buildings are also places, not merely lines or interfaces with no thickness or presence themselves; hence we need benches, galleries, balconies, places to sit, walls perhaps that weave in and out to create alcoves (even the appropriate depth of such niches is calculated: six feet). Domestic gardens or some other literally outdoor room (trellises, sliding or canvas roofs) should be built.[9] There is an argument for fruit trees and orchards, which in places "give the land an almost magical identity," like the cherry trees of Japan and the olive groves of Greece. Trees of all sorts are vital. We remember their psychological freight: in dreams, for example, trees are often symbols for the wholeness of personality. ("Since . . . psychic growth . . . happens involuntarily and naturally, it is in dreams frequently symbolized by the tree, whose slow, powerful, involuntary growth fulfills a definite pattern."[10] The night after writing this, I dreamed about oak trees: branching, gnarled, rough-bark oaks, the kind that flowed from my mother's paintbrush as age drew upon her.) But trees cannot be just randomly spread around either. Different kinds and arrangments of trees create different kinds of places. Alexander even proposes a typology: umbrellas (a single spreading tree that defines an outdoor room); a pair (a gateway, perhaps?); groves; squares; avenues. Placing trees in meaningful patterns and places also makes it particularly likely that they will be cherished and cared for, not just by some public works department, but by their neighborhood. Yet again, flower and shrub gardens should be grown, should be planned to go partly wild, should be walled or partly walled, should be trellised, might include greenhouses, edible plants, should include seats for solitude or the conversation of a few.[11]

Notice once again that we are not talking about massive, sweeping, top-down social changes but of tinkering with zoning requirements, building or retrofitting our houses in small ways that may take time, like the shrubs that may take a generation to grow up to create half-hidden gardens. The "timeless way of building" also *takes* time; that is part of its adaptability. But the possibilities are overwhelming: the world is crowded with them. This can hardly be stressed enough. I cite so many examples not to offer any kind of summary—one can't, the work is far too rich—but rather to underline yet again how many possibilities there are, how much undeveloped potential there is right around us, right now.

Other entire realms of architectural inquiry cannot even be discussed here, such as the ancient arts of *siting* buildings, perfected by the Greek temple builders, according to Vincent Scully's extraordinarily sensitive and scholarly studies, as well, half a world away, as by ancient Chinese geomancers, under the heading of "Feng Shui"—viewing the land as "a network of potent spots connected by lines of energy."[12] Biologist Lyall Watson writes of this worldwide geomancy:

> You have only to compare the sites they [the geomancers] chose with others selected more recently by purely secular considerations. The old ones have a mood and balance which is unmistakable. They occupy positions of advantage; these need not be prominent in the sense that they straddle the highest hills, but they always lie at the focal point of an area. At a point where physical and spiritual forces combine to produce emotional equilibrium.[13]

Animals, he says, sense such spots too; animals and humans often seem to pick the same spots of repose, and even insect swarms apparently respond to them.[14] But enough. Once again, the speculations and the stories may carry us away. It is all we can do here to open some doors.

Another set of proposals. Millions of Americans already garden. Suppose that many more of us did. In "quiet zones" or not—this is a mostly independent proposal; in rural communes or behind downtown brownstones; communally or so privately that even the neighbors don't know. Suppose that we grew flowers, grew food, grew herbs, but grew *something*. Would it change us?

Some people will reject the possibility up front, especially those who have never gardened, and those for whom environmental crisis, like all the other familiar "crises" of our time, requires draconian, massive, and top-down solutions. What you learn in a garden is subtle and not necessarily clear from the near side. It is probably harder to recognize than the values of quiet zones or earth-rooted buildings. But it is also crucial. And here too, it turns out, we are speaking of "contact," a possibility that is modest and once again right next to us.

Gardening from the start throws us into a partly human, partly more-than-human region, where the usual assumptions are worn down and something more complex emerges. For one thing, good gardening requires attentiveness. Attentiveness to the nature of the soil, to the smallest particularities of place (not "landscape," not something so general as "the ecology," but maybe, primarily, fifty or two hundred square feet of ground). Attentiveness to the patterns of the weather, planting crops with different cold tolerance at the appropriate times in the spring, watching the frosts in the fall and the heat and rain in summer, judging what plants need to be covered or picked depending on how hard a frost is upon you, paying attention to what is grown successfully in the area. Attentiveness to the patterns of sun and shade on a particular spot, and correspondingly to the leafing cycles of trees. In North Carolina we can almost grow an entire crop of spring vegetables—snow peas, lettuce, onions—before the trees leaf in and shade the back garden; but it does mean planting in January, always under threat of frost, watching the skies. Attentiveness, finally, to the needs of whole communities of living things, finicky and at times demanding: only at the end does the garden, quite literally, "bear fruit." Gardens require care, on their own schedule and their own great cycles: welcome, ground preparation, planting, watering, weeding, harvesting, farewell, and preparation for winter. Growing two and even three crops of certain foods complicates the cycles and the calendar of imperatives still further. The very cadence of life is more-than-human: "a beat in step with the seasons."[15]

Even the best of gardens remains vulnerable to the extremes, to Earth's unpredictable forces: sudden storms, long droughts, the surprise freeze; enormous and horrendously specialized insects, like tomato hornworm, which appear as if by magic just when they can do the maximum damage, but then two days later are sucked dry by a thousand little parasites that just as magically appear. You don't need to retreat to the wild to encounter nature's power. Holding the season's first ripe tomato in your hand, you feel a little as if some kind of gem fell into your hand, utterly improbably, out of some enormous heavenly contention, most of which you remain unaware of. Getting anything at all is a humbling gift.

Still, the overall feeling, gardening, is not that the Earth stands at a distance, unpredictable and violent. Buried in dirt and horse manure, I recognize a richer truth. I am, again, *part* of the Earth, in the simplest and most concrete way. In the garden I belong to a multispecies community of certain plants and insects and animals, in league against others. There are the plants themselves, obviously, for whom I am a means to flourishing and perhaps reproduction, their ally and retainer, the minor matter of my borrowing some fruit notwithstanding. But the community is also much larger. Myself and my family, our friends and dinner guests, the soup kitchen that gets our overproduction, the dogs that help turn the compost, the birds and spiders and wasps that control their pestiferous cousins, and on and on; all of us in league with the plants against those other insects, and the deer (alas), and the kid down the hill who lobs baseballs into the corn. Finally even species lines are redrawn. *This* is "contact" in practice: not some kind of abstract appreciation, but considering the parasitized hornworm with a comradely eye, dropping hair snippets to deter the deer, and, as one of our neighbors recommends, urinating around the garden—she claims, conveniently, that only male urine will do: imagine the scene around the neighborhood on certain spring evenings—to hold the line against the rabbits.

Turning the compost, thinking of both the meals these dregs made possible and the meals they soon will make possible again. It is to experience ourselves as part of larger wholes, simply, directly, in and through one's *body*.

Oh yes, to be sure, gardens are "ecological"—the tomatoes are healthier and are not shipped halfway across the country to taste like cardboard in your salad; and there are the undeniable satisfactions of having brought a crop to fruition. All these things matter. But there are mysteries and rejoinings here that carry us so much farther still! Editor and gardener Michael Pollan, in a recent book, describes gardens as a "middle space" between the utterly humanized and the wild. The book is called *Second Nature*: gardens are not "first nature," not *in*human; we are speaking of a *more*-than-human space in which we both act and are acted upon. A long, slow dance with sun and seed and deer.

And time. The domestication of plants was the beginning of settled civilization. In a sense, they domesticated *us*. Everything we now eat is a product of long practice and experiment, even world traveling and disaster. Indian vegetables—tomato, potato, yam, maize; even these *names* are Indian, as are hominy, squash, avocado, papaya, tapioca, scuppernong—discovered by Europeans in America, imported to Europe and then re-exported back to the Americas. Some rose varieties can be traced back to the fifteenth century. Proponents of different rose varieties have been debating for almost as long, and countless experiments have been tried. Even our weeds have histories. Saint John's-wort was brought to America in 1696 by Rosicrucians to exorcise evil spirits. Dandelions arrived with colonists who prized them as salad greens. Tumbleweed came to South Dakota with a group of Ukrainian immigrants; they brought it with their flax seeds.[16] Weeping willows, widely regarded as a "weed" tree on account of its fast growth and its unfriendliness to basements, is an eighteenth-century garden import, brought to America by Samuel

Johnson, first president of Columbia University (then King's College), who saw it in Alexander Pope's famous garden on the Thames and brought back one shoot to his home along Connecticut's Housatonic River, from which it promptly escaped.

"Weeds are us," as Pollan puts it.[17] Even weeds that are the gardener's bane exist in a symbiotic relation precisely with gardens. They don't grow everywhere, despite their reputation: not in prairies, not in forests, but in places that humans have created by altering or eliminating the existing plant communities: vacant lots, railroad cuts, lawns, and, yes, gardens. Every gardener knows the uncanny ability of any newly turned piece of ground to produce exact weed replicas of whatever vegetables you plant in it: pea imposters in the peas, carrot frauds in the carrots. Maybe imposter seeds are more likely in seed batches of whatever they imitate; or maybe the other weeds just get pulled up sooner, though this alone cannot be the explanation—there are no carrot imposters in the peas. At any rate, the effect remains uncanny. Some imposters actually change their appearance to imitate whatever crop they come up among ("Wild oats growing in a field of alternating rows of spring and winter barley will imitate the habits of either crop *depending on the row*. When one rice mimic became so troublesome that researchers planted a purple variety of rice to expose the weeds once and for all, within a few years the weed-rice had turned purple too.")[18] Weeds are so versatile and familiar that Euell Gibbons became famous for insisting, plausibly, that American cuisine take advantage of them.[19]

Pollan draws what he calls a "new environmental ethic" out of the gardener's practice—an ethic quite different from the familiar, philosophically sweeping "ethics" based on wilderness. First, a gardener's outlook is emphatically, persistently, necessarily local. It gives different answers in different places, instead of imposing some single overall model. Discovering them may take many generations, and they always need renewing. "Heirloom" (nonhybrid) seed growers encourage their customers to seek out neighbors and "old-timers" to help recover the local gardening knowledge that is being lost.[20]

Gardeners also accept contingency, tolerate uncertainty. You expect wild variations of rain, climate, insects, sun within which you seek what regularity you can. Gardeners are unromantic ("Perhaps that's why garden writing tends to be comic, rather than lyrical or elegaic in the way that nature writing usually is: the gardener can never quite forget about the rug underfoot [that nature might at any time pull out], the possibility of the offstage hook."). Gardeners are *active*—I return to this point in a moment; and optimistic, in the sense that gardeners must believe that their impact on nature can be constructive.[21]

And gardens, crucially, live in the "middle:" they are "an indissoluble mix of our culture and whatever it is that's really out there." Here, unmistakably, humans are not the whole story: we are included in a more-than-human enterprise. On this point Pollan joins a long tradition in American thinking about nature. Tony Hiss lists a wide range of terms that have been used for, as it were, gardened landscapes: places where just such "mixes" have shaped the land as a whole. The terms: intermediate landscape, working countryside, working landscape, managed landscape, humanized landscape, historic landscape, ancient landscape (the English high pastures, for instance, cleared six thousand years ago for animals), cultural landscape, heritage landscape.

> These are all terms that have been coined over the years by botanists, landscape historians, sociologists, historical ecologists, and other specialists who have studied both the history and future of the countryside in order to distinguish two different kinds of terrain—natural landscapes, which . . . are those parts of the countryside that human beings haven't altered or interfered with; and landscapes whose function and look, or character, or feel, have

been shaped over time by human activities as much as by natural processes.[22]

Coevolved places: places whose shape is a joint product; places of human presence and activity but not domination; places that constitute or at least live within "margins." Remember that term of Wendell Berry's; it comes from his own gardenlike practice, maintaining a small farm. Mowing his hayfield with a team of horses, Berry encounters a hawk who lands quite close to him, watching carefully but without fear. The hawk comes, he says, "because of the conjunction of the small pasture and its wooded borders, of open hunting ground and the security of trees. . . . The human eye itself seems drawn to such margins, hungering for the difference made in the countryside by a hedgy fencerow, a stream, or a grove of trees. These margins are biologically rich, the meeting of two kinds of habitat."[23] The hawk would not have come, he says, if the field had been larger, or if there had been no trees, or if he had been plowing with a tractor. "Intermediate" spaces are those inhabited and maintained by humans who understand, with Berry, that a certain *scale* to the fields, and even the avoidance of machinery, may be essential to "contact." "Intermediate" space, understood this way, has a point: to remain mindfully within the more-than-human, not totally to transform and finally desolate the land.

This theme is not new either, yet it is persistently misunderstood. Regardless of what I say, I sometimes feel that any talk of "contact" will be misunderstood as implying some sort of passivity, as if we can only open to the world like a flower and let it come to us. But this is as clearly as possible *not* the case with gardening or with Berry's farming or with Alexander's ways of building. It's not even true of flowers, actually. These are active practices, forms of engagement: open-ended but not somehow passively just "open." They are persistently *interactive*. Even

Thoreau, who we often seem to imagine in some kind of purely contemplative attitude, vegetating day after day by the Walden shore, had departed much farther from the sort of Emersonian romanticism that was content with contemplation of nature at a distance. Thoreau spent most of his life as a surveyor and amateur ecologist. *Walden* is full of biological and limnological observations, and at his death he left a 400-page manuscript, only recently published, on the ecology of the seed. He surveyed, he practiced a kind of protoecological theory and investigation. *Walden* is mostly an account of his *treks*: he "surveyed" in many ways.

The other tempting misconstruction of "contact" is, oddly enough, exactly the opposite: the supposition that *only* activity is meant here, that there is no space for contemplation or thinking at all. But Berry, for one, is both farmer and philosopher at once, and in fact it is his farming that makes his philosophy so good. It is nothing so simple as that he thinks while he plows, as if we must insist on the unbridgeable dividedness of "theory" and "practice" come what may. Instead, his plowing, his maintenance of this kind of farm, his attentiveness to *this* place, is precisely a form of thinking as well. (Why is it so hard for us to imagine the two together, in fact as necessary to each other?) Put the image of Berry horse-plowing his small fields alongside the acrimonious and abstract philosophical debate about the concept of "nature." Here the best-known positions are the extremes. "Social ecologists" insist that no environment is ever purely natural and that the challenge is really to get our humanization of the world under socially progressive and politically inclusive control. Some "deep ecologists," meanwhile, argue that only wilderness is the "real world."[24] Both views have something to offer. But it may be that only from the point of view of a genuine practice, even so simple a practice as gardening or the attempt to create "quiet places" or maintain "margins," might we finally achieve the necessary experience to take what we can from the purely philosophical debate, and also to go beyond it toward a better set of questions and answers. One view insists on an inhuman ideal, the other on a wholly human ideal. It is the *intermediate* space that is missing. What we need to explore are the possible realms of interaction. Precisely the maintenance of something like "margins" emerges as part of the answer.

Also not to be misunderstood: I do not mean that there should not be "practices of the wild," to use Gary Snyder's term, or that we should not try to preserve all of the wilderness that we still can save. Wilderness—that which lies on the other side of the "margin"—is absolutely essential, even for the vitality of margins themselves. Eight-thousand-year-old bristlecones, three-thousand-year-old redwoods; the genuinely inhuman presence of grizzly or whale or eel or alpine lichen: these things must live wholly outside the human sphere. Instead of building ever-wider roads to the greatest places of power, destroying or trivializing them in the process, it is those very places that need to be left, or made, relatively inaccessible. To reach them a pilgrim must enter a domain that is *not* our own, to sleep on the earth, walk through unarmored, for days and nights and weeks perhaps, guided by dreams, or the stories of previous pilgrims. Hans Peter Duerr argues that it is precisely the existence of the "other side," of real alternatives as well as dream spaces and symbolic spaces beyond civilization, that made civilization tolerable for traditional cultures and even in medieval Europe.[25]

Yes. Yet it is all too tempting to imagine that the practice of the wild, or wild places themselves, exist entirely off the continuum of the rest of our lives, and that wilderness alone is what any "deep" environmentalism worthy of the name must address. I think we need to stress, instead, the connections. Snyder himself decries the tendency to separate certain areas as "sacred" while consigning the rest, as the natural reflex of our conception of the sacred, to exploitation and desolation. "For a people of an old culture, *all* their mutually owned territory holds numinous life and spirit." Certain places, he says, have a higher "spiritual density" than others because of "plant or animal habitat intensities, or associations with legend, or connections with human totemic ancestry, or because of geomorphological anomaly." But all have some.[26] We need to remember this. Farm country, too, holds a richness of meanings that can make it "numinous" with a cultural light. "Margins," as described by Berry, like hedgerows or riverbanks, may offer a "high spiritual density" precisely because of "plant or animal habitat intensities," sometimes requiring human maintenance. Human maintenance is not incompatible with their essence. Snyder in the end finds wildness everywhere ("ineradicable populations of fungi, moss, mold, yeasts, and such that surround and inhabit us; deer mice on the back porch, deer bounding across the freeway, pigeons in the park, spiders in the corners . . . , bacteria in our loam and in our yogurt.").[27] Perhaps at this extreme we do lose a valid distinction that the term "wild" makes; certainly there are distinctive and necessary ways in which the senses are engaged in relatively unhumanized and relatively quiet and dark places. The back porch will not always do. Yet it must *mostly* do. In the end we all must follow Snyder back from the iconic wild into the "intermediate" spaces, human but more-than-human too, where almost all of us, almost all the time, *live*. Ultimately, if the great offerings of the wild—the quiet and the dark; the other creatures and the solitude—are not possible right "next to us," they will not be possible at all.

Wilderness is not one single type of thing. It is an entire continuum of possibilities, sizes, shapes, prospects. Writer Bill McKibben, a resident of the Adirondacks, proposes the Adirondack region as a kind of laboratory *intermediate* space, as a testing ground for co-inhabitation. The real issue raised by our destruction of wilderness, he writes, "is that we have yet, anywhere, to learn to live in and around nature without wrecking it." That is what we need to learn—and the Adirondacks, he argues, could be one place to begin to learn it.

> More than anything else, because so much nature is in these mountains and so few people, they offer a chance to nurture the idea that there should be limits to how humans live. This question of limits—which has important implications not only for property use but for how we transport ourselves, how many children we bear, what we eat, how much we consume—is the question of the next century. The current dichotomy, where wilderness is only imaginable behind a fence, encourages the idea that in the "normal" human world we can do as we please.[28]

We could think even bigger. Sweeping open-space wildlife sanctuaries have been proposed, like the "Buffalo Commons," a mosaic of sparsely populated and already largely federally owned or federally subsidized lands on the Great Plains. They too would be inhabited—or rather, co-inhabited—and governed, perhaps, by the indigenous peoples.[29] Other wildernesses might well be uninhabited by humans—perhaps even off-limits to humans: buffered by surrounding, more accessible lands.

My general theme, though, is what we really need right now is to think in the opposite and much less familiar direction: to think *smaller*. *Pocket* wilderness. Wildness right next to us. Maybe, for one thing, we need to return to the gardner's give and take, as Pollan insists, but with more give and less take. Sara Stein, in her new book on gardening, argues for a return to native plants, for letting the lawn and woods go wild, for regenerating the old habitats undone by our obsession with neatening and homogenizing the land and growing food only for ourselves. Tiny wet areas nourish the frogs, native berry bushes feed the birds, dead snags feed the bugs, and the bugs feed the woodpeckers. Stein's visitors go home with wildflowers. ("Who would ask for a bouquet of lawn?")[30] It is possible in the backyard—Stein cites blueprints[31]—or down the street. Hedgerows and stream edges. On a slightly larger scale, city parks and greenways. Streets for walking.

Walking: another theme. The last chapter spoke of the ways in which speed cuts us off from more-than-human worlds: homogenizing space (standardization of highways makes for safety, familiarity, and hence boredom everywhere); turning animals into "road kill;" obliterating most of the sounds and smells of the land, as well as most of the sights. You must constantly watch the road, and besides almost everything is going by too fast to look at anyway. ("The particular features of terrain are whirled up in a passing cloud. . . . No time is allowed for the slow weaving of associations, tying the mysteries of human life to a certain tree along the road, a half-fallen stone wall.")[32] The car also makes us physically almost immobile: our bodies barely move.

But to *walk* is to feel the winds, hear the birds and other animals, to return to the body, to *be* an animal. It is to reopen closed-off possibilities of encounter. It is to remember that the world is generally *not* sharp edged and yes or no:

> the walk liberating, I was released from forms,
> from the perpendiculars,
>   straight lines, blocks, boxes, binds
> of thought
> into the hues, shadings, rises, flowing bends and blends
>   of sight . . .[33]

That this is perfectly obvious does not keep us from ignoring it almost all the time. I barely notice the fall trees along my own street unless I walk the street. Never mind that I drive it two or six times a day. Some things take the leisured eye to see, undivided and unhurried attention, like the changing texture of fall trees, for some reason very marked this year, with their brazenly varied leaf colors giving the masses of woods much sharper dimensions than summer's clumps of indistinguishable greens; now they are more like rock formations in the sun; and then a few weeks later they are the most delicate and modest, still wearing a few leaves, while the birds flutter and dance, even at noon, and the neighborhood looks like a Chinese landscape painting. From the car it is all invisible, and inaudible, or else looks like some kind of subway tunnel, and I am tense, fixated on whereever I am going, somewhere else.

Much more might also be said about the character of *places* under the regime of the car compared to the practice (Thoreau actually says "art") of walking. It would not be surprising if our practices feed back to shape our places in turn, in yet another kind of self-validating reduction. Consider, for example, what the displacement of walking by driving did to the lawn. Pollan argues that lawns have become placeless, utterly insensitive to place—they all look the same, broad expanses of turf grasses, none of which, it turns out, are even native to North America. (Lawns drink, he complains, "from the national stream of images, lift our gaze from the real places we live and fix it on unreal places elsewhere. Lawns are a form of television.")[34] They are also, he argues, a direct response to the rise of the motorcar, and the residential spaces the car shaped, the suburb. The lawn is designed for the sweeping passing view, a view that has no time for dense detail but prefers the restful flowing-together lines of the open lawns gently bordering the street. And this is the view, of course, of the motorist. Lawns are a generalized form of *parkway*. To let the lawn go wild, to return it to meadow or some more fine-grained use, for one thing, reasserts the primacy of walking speed, even loitering speed. Like Pollan's new environmental ethics of the garden, it requires again more attention to local conditions. Berry again: "The question that must be addressed . . . is not how to care for the planet, but how to care for each of the planet's millions of human and natural neighborhoods, each of its millions of small pieces and parcels of land, each one of which is in some precious way different from all the others. Our understandable wish to preserve the planet must somehow be reduced to the scale of our competence."[35] My own neighborhood, built along a narrow street twistingly paralleling a stream, leaving most of the tulip poplars and loblolly pines untouched, now is slowly evolving into a fine-grained, detailed flow, one thickly planted front yard giving way to a garden space in the slightly higher and sunnier yard of the next, then to ivy or woods or fruit trees or another garden. That this is a *walking* street is no coincidence. It invites walking, it rewards walking, its flow is a walker's flow, and as a result a walker's perspective is coming to shape it.

Such a neighborhood is also a "margin:" a place open to encounter. Frogs and owls and possums live here, as well as the usual raccoons and squirrels and rabbits. Human presence at walking speed returns to the benign. Walkers do not squash animals: there is no equivalent to road kill along walking paths. Instead, it is possible actually to encounter another animal, a real creature with its own ways, possibly even a creature (if I pass the same way often) whose home I come to know, who becomes a kind of friend as I pass on my own way. My kids may follow animal trails back to to their haunts, learn to walk in the woods. My running route, stream and city greenway only a few yards wide at some points, still hosts bluebirds, kingfishers, even the occasional heron.

To improve walking, as Alexander points out, requires footpaths, and the farther from the noise and danger of cars the better. Imagine it: cities could be transformed, new and more dense public spaces might arise. The countryside too will change, as we create more "country fingers," as Alexander calls them. Connected fingers of land, barely inhabited, not intensively farmed or otherwise used and remade, a kind of migration corridor for the human saunterer as well as the animal populations that are at present being dismembered and isolated along with their habitats. Planners and conceptual artists Helen and Newt Harrison argue that the required changes are, once again, not enormous. It takes restoring some traditional farmland, letting some meadows grow back into woods, securing some corridors that in many cases already exist, like abandoned railroad rights-of-way (now in some states being preserved for bikeways)—though the Harrisons also suggest some wilder new strategies too, like throwing hundred-yard-wide viaducts over roads and rivers to carry forest and forest paths across what otherwise might be insuperable barriers.[36]

Precedents, inspirations, even parts of a legal structure for a "green mosaic" already exist. Britain's system of public access to footpaths, distinct from the roads, secured by common-law rights now many centuries old and coupled with the relative compactness of towns and the abruptness of the country–town borders, makes the English countryside far more readily available, far more naturally a part of people's lives. Finland has a similar system. In America there is no parallel legal structure, but there are certainly parallel practices. In the small-town Wisconsin of my youth, none of the local farmers thought twice if you walked across their fields. Robert Bendick, former director of Rhode Island's Department of Environmental Management, explained Rhode Islanders' striking commitment to open-space protection by citing very similar practices: "According to their own code of the countryside, an informal, unwritten tradition that was nevertheless widely acknowledged and accepted around the state, landowners of the farms and forests and shorelines of Rhode Island gave their neighbors the use of these places, so that private property functioned—very discretely—as public open space."[37]

This tradition, itself perhaps a holdover from the English traditions the first Rhode Islanders brought with them, is eroding as building pressures on the land increase and new owners come in, heedless of the traditions of the state. Now there is increasing formal public action to preserve open space. Bendick also launched a program to identify and preserve little pockets of relatively undeveloped land, often naturally "protected," like river valleys, and sometimes hardly visible even to the residents.[38]

So we need more intermediate space, more accessible intermediate space, and a clearer awareness of such places as a distinct and essential kind of space. We are still tempted to think that walking in a relatively uninterrupted and open-ended way is possible only in officially designated parks or wilderness, where of course we must have all the equipment and experience to backpack, while everywhere else it must be only some kind of exercise, and rather inefficient at that, certainly as a way of getting anywhere. Intermediate spaces save walking as a kind of *contact*. Benton MacKaye, the forester and planner who originally proposed the Appalachian Trail, in fact imagined that trail not as a totally wild and separate route but as one part of a grander system whose aim was to open and connect precisely the "mixed," rural landscapes that, MacKaye believed, we need to share and to love in order to live with a true sense of connectedness and harmony.[39]

And in fact, despite the Appalachian Trail's reputation as a wilderness trail, that is actually what it does. Of course there are the mountaintops and long wild sections. But the trail also regularly follows old woods roads and even some not-so-old paved roads. It parallels navigated rivers and railroads. A meadow just off the trail in the Pisgah doubles as an airfield. Quaint little Wawayanda Village in New Jersey was, in the 1850s, a smelter town, smogged in and denuded of trees for miles around. Roan Mountain in North Carolina is a former Catskill-style resort, of which no buildings remain; what is left is a mountainside crowded with rhododendron and azaleas gone wild. Three miles away you might have spent the night in a barn next to a solitary old farmhouse, looking down a long mountain valley. The farmhouse has now been remade, two-dimensionalized actually, for a movie set, then abandoned; the notebooks at nearby trail lean-tos offered some commentary on this development when I leafed through them one night. I don't remember the name of the movie. Farms, fields, houses, sometimes hostels adjoin the trail. Somewhere in New Jersey, so it is said, there lies buried treasure from an old bank. At Watuga Lake Dam (the TVA accompanies you on the Trail through much of the South), the lean-to offers a Gideon Bible, from which I once spent a rainy October afternoon reading aloud the Book of Revelation.

The Appalachian Trail, in short, is a walk through back-country America and its history, emphatically a "mixed" kind of space. To recognize it as such, I think, would make it easier to save the similar "mixed" places that are now under pressure all around us, places too often abandoned to the tender mercies of the "developer" because they are not "wild."

I suppose I should add that neither walking nor anything else proposed here is meant as somehow mandatory for everyone. The imperative is to create the *space* for walking within the otherwise madly onrushing automotive culture: to make walking, real walking, an option at least for some people, some communities, to rediversify our alternatives from the current *one.* For cars do have a monopoly at present: their sound goes everywhere, their fumes fill everyone's air (the average car produces its own weight in carbon monoxide every year), there is hardly anywhere one can walk or bicycle without having to deal with cars, and meanwhile many of the places one might go are themselves located for the convenience of the car. Grocery stores settle in satellite shopping malls, for example, that are virtually inaccessible in any other way. And it is not so difficult to make other ways of getting around possible, to allow them to recover a little of their original sense and reward, and to see what will grow out of that. Some cities are already banning cars from city centers, since there at least they are obviously dysfunctional even for the people who use them. Movements are afoot to reclaim at least some roads for biking and walking a few days a month—even such "country" roads as the Blue Ridge Parkway. Plans for the city "after the car" already exist. Christopher Alexander and his colleagues, naturally, have a few dozen.[40]

Quiet zones, margins, new kinds of houses, new kinds of cities, gardens, walking: all of these are still only a few possibilities out of many, and, I know, are only developed in the briefest way here. I am not trying to offer blueprints. It is in the nature of the case that no blueprints are possible. What we need now, as I said in opening this chapter, is a range of beginnings. These are some beginnings. Let me conclude with one more set of proposals in a rather different key.

Think of how many of the origins of our divisions of time lie in natural rhythms. Our year is the Earth's journey around the Sun. The month is named for the moon. The week's seven days are named for the seven celestial wanderers known to the ancient geocentric world (Saturday for Saturn, Thursday for Jupiter, Sunday for Sun). Native Americans have evocative names for all the year's moons: "Long Nights Moon" or "Popping Trees Moon" in December; "Harvest" or "Fruit" Moon; the "Frosty Moon" of November, "Sap" or "Awakening" Moon in March. The ancient Near Eastern civilizations, all dependent on and acutely aware of the growing cycles, held their great festivals on the Solstices and Equinoxes—Litha, Mabon, Eostar, Yule—and also celebrated the points midway between.

Dimly and at a distance, then, our own great festivals draw us back to the old cycles of light and dark, the seasons and the stars.

Christmas, Christianity's (re)birth festival, at Winter Solstice, the rebirth of the light. Hannukah, the Jewish festival of light, at the very moment that the year gets the darkest: the twenty-fifth of Kislev, in the Jewish lunar calendar; the waning of the moon closest to Winter Solstice; thus the day of the darkest moon and the shortest sun; the day the Maccabees reconsecrated the recaptured Temple in Jerusalem, chosen because this was the day that the Hellenizers desecrated it, which in turn was chosen perhaps because twenty-fifth of December was already a Roman holiday—the (re)birthday of the Unconquerable Sun.[41] Birth and rebirth: the return of the light. In early Spring, the bawdy Christian carnivals (from *carne vale:* "farewell to meat," before the Lenten fasting). Jewish Purim, likewise a carnival, hilarity, release. Easter—Eostar—Passover, at the Spring Equinox: resurrection, escape from bondage, as the Earth truly bursts into new life, maple buds swelling in the newly warm wind. May Day is the following midpoint day, halfway between Spring Equinox and Summer Solstice, anciently called "Beltane." Ancient "Samhain," midway between Fall Equinox and Winter Solstice, became All Saints Day, its eve, All Hallows Eve: Halloween. The death festival, as the leaves fall and the darkness descends. No light without dark, no life without death. Then Thanksgiving, the harvest festival; then the year renews itself.

Suppose that we take it upon ourselves to re-root our festivals explicitly in the natural and pagan soil from which they sprang, and to elaborate new nature-centered festivals and practices where at present we have none. I mean *festivals*, too, not simply "vacations"; literally empty time, time not committed to something else. No, something more like "holidays," true communal celebrations, literally *"holy* days," except I do not mean "holy" in the usual religious sense; instead, special days, festive days, collectively shared ritual times, like we already have in Thanksgiving and Halloween, but now with their natural origins recognized and deepened. Reaffirmed. The very term *pagan* derives from the Latin for country dweller. Suppose that, experientially, it really is that simple. The country: that is, places where the cycles of light and dark are still present to the senses, where growing seasons matter, where the moon can still overcome you walking out the door. Where pumpkins ripen for Halloween, where lilies bloom for Eostar, where the long, long days and long, long nights can be felt. In such places, the old festivals are still new, still the right gestures, every year.

We could also imagine any number of new practices. Already at New Year's many people all across the country traipse out, before dawn, to count birds for the Audubon Society. We might institutionalize "Bird Count Day." Imagine weeks of preparation by eager schoolchildren learning to identify birds. Imagine the hopefulness of the observers that a rare bird might come their way, like amateur astronomers hoping to discover a comet. Imagine "Star Nights" on which all lights everywhere are turned out, not just in the dark/quiet zones; these could be timed to coincide with meteor showers, eclipses, occlusions. The poet Antler recalls Emerson's epiphany—"If the stars came out only one night in a thousand years, how people would believe and adore, and preserve from generation to generation, remembrance of the miracle they'd been shown"—and imagines the scene:

> Whole populations thronging to darkened
> baseball stadiums and skyscrapertops
> to sit holding hands en masse
> and look up at the billion-year spree
> of the realm of the nebulae![42]

For us, it is there every clear night: the right festivals could teach us all to see it.

We might coordinate other festivals with the great animal migrations: whales, salmon, hawks, warblers. We might move

New Year's back to the Spring, where it was for the entire ancient world until the medieval popes moved it to the dead of winter precisely to break the pagan connection. (There's the counter-theme: the two-millennium-old assault on paganism as a profoundly, necessarily *urban* phenomenon. Streetlights and noise are only the latest weapon.) We might take that once-in-four-years twenty-ninth day, added to February to compensate (some of) the slippage between the Gregorian calendar and the actual year, and turn it into a celebration of nature's elusiveness—of precisely the real world's *ungraspability* in any of our counting schemes. What a thoughtlessly wasted opportunity for a holiday! Let us leave it a day "in between"—a day out of time—precisely *not* a calendar day like any other, but a day that does not have a number, therefore a day when business perforce must stop, when not even the most Gordian knot of lawyers can help us, a day when all our certainties might find it wise to follow their lead and stay at home—a day for dancing in the streets.

We might set aside nights each month on which we simply pay attention to the Moon. *Real* Monday (Moon-day), so to speak. We might have a night each month on which all newcomers to this Earth are introduced to it, a kind of baptism into the living community that is the Earth. Ecofeminist philosopher Charlene Spretnak describes what many of us have tried to do, furtively perhaps, in recent years. This is paganism—in the original sense—in practice:

> When my daughter was about three days old and we were still in the hospital, I wrapped her up one evening and slipped outside to a little garden in the warmth of late June. I introduced her to the pine trees and the plants and the flowers, and they to her, and finally to the pearly moon wrapped in a soft haze and to the stars. I . . . had felt an impulse for my wondrous little child to meet the rest of cosmic society.[43]

Spretnak goes on: "that experience, although lovely and rich, was so disconnected from life in a modern, technocratic society that I soon forgot all about it." She only remembered it when she began practicing ecofeminism. But how profoundly right the impulse! Imagine how powerful, how connected, could be a culture that once again systematized and practiced such responses: that once again pays attention. No longer furtive and readily forgotten impulses, departures from the consensual, rationalized patterns within which we now think we live, but the communally shared, ever-deepening pattern of the month and the year and of one's life itself. We long for the time when such celebrations come naturally, shared by all one's friends and family, the emotional culminations of the community's year, not peculiar and individually sustained interruptions in a collective calendar imposed by the dead hands of antipagans millennia old.

To come back to our senses: to pay attention. Too often we think of "paying attention" as a mental act, as if the mind is a kind of searchlight, a beam that can be focussed anywhere and illuminates whatever it is shone upon. Perhaps sometimes this is even true. But when it comes to our life within the more-than-human, it would be better to think of ourselves as more like fish in the sea. Paying attention is not so much a matter of focus as it is of *immersion*: of living in the presence of the more-than-human. That is the point of quiet zones and gardens and walking and festivals: not so much to "focus" on what lies beyond us, episodic and glancing as any such attention would have to be, but to live in its presence, constantly, to awake and go to sleep with it, to take its rhythms and cycles for the rhythms and cycles of your own life, until the two finally merge into one stream. To meet the moon at three days old, to hear owl and whippoorwill through the night, to think of Halloween when we plant pumpkins in the long days of June. *Then* we have truly come back to our senses; then we are truly "back to Earth."

7

Transhuman Etiquettes

Animal trainer and writer Vicki Hearne visits an animal training facility to observe Washoe, one of the chimps trained to use American Sign Language. She ends up observing the people instead.

There were roughly three categories of people going in and out of the main compound. There was the group that included trainers, handlers, and caretakers, there were Hollywood types of one sort and another and there were academics who were there mostly because of the presence of the signing chimpanzees. I realized that I was able, without consciously thinking about it, accurately and from several hundred yards away to identify which group anyone who came in belonged to. . . .

The handlers, I noticed, walked in with a soft, acute, 380-degree awareness: they were receptively establishing . . . acknowledgment of and relationships with all of the several hundred pumas, wolves, chimps, spider monkeys and Galapagos tortoises. Their ways of moving *fit* into the spaces shaped by the animals' awareness.

The Hollywood types moved . . . with vast indifference to where they were and might as well have been on an interior set with flats painted with pictures of tortoises or on the stage of a Las Vegas nightclub. They were psychically intrusive, and I remembered Dick Koehler [an animal trainer and writer] saying that you could count on your thumbs the number of actors, directors and so on who could actually respond meaningfully to what an animal is doing.

The academics didn't strut in quite that way, but they were

nonetheless psychically intrusive and failed to radiate the intelligence the handlers did. . . . They had too many questions, too many hidden assumptions about their roles as observer. I am talking about nice, smart people, but good handlers don't "observe" animals in this way, . . . with that stare that makes almost all animals a bit uneasy.[1]

I bet that they were *all* nice, smart people. Some of the Hollywood types, too, were surely vegetarians or users of cruelty-free cosmetics. Many of the academics probably had pets. Yet only a few established some kind of relationship with the animals. The rest—most—did not. Being "nice" (or believing yourself "nice") is not enough. Something else, perhaps something radically different in kind, is necessary.

Ah, yes, we say, we know this. Some people just "have a way with animals." Some lucky people have the magic touch. Thus we neatly excuse ourselves from asking whether there is something much more ordinary that accounts for the difference in animals' responses. Suppose there is? Even the most ordinary abilities look magical to people who lack them, and precisely to consider them "magical" is one sure way to keep yourself from thinking them through more carefully or developing them yourself. Perhaps we even ought to say that they *are* magical, but then magic itself, real magic, is not something that somehow descends on some of us by grace alone. Maybe the story is a little different.

"Relationship"—mutual responsiveness with other animals—requires, for starters, *acknowledgment.* And acknowledgment, despite its depth and difficulty, is not a mystery. There are no secrets. There is no simple, irrevocable grace or dis-grace. We can even take it apart and look at it bit by bit. Such is our reduced and skeptical state, now, that perhaps we must.

For one thing, acknowledgment usually includes some sort of verbal offering or exchange: speaking at least a word or two. *What* is said, though, what statement is made, matters not at all. We say "How are you?" half the time without expecting or even wanting a response. We talk to babies, completely without self-consciousness, though we know that the "content" of what we say is meaningless to them, again for the sake of connection through sound, emotional overtone, aquaintance. Caught up in our preoccupation with propositional language, we forget that the simple making of sounds, quite apart from their "content," is a form of assurance, emotional linkage, social bonding. Bateson suggests, remember, that cetaceans may have so richly elaborated this "relational" function of verbalization that *we* are the ones unspeakably primitive by comparison. Other animals elaborate other forms: tail wagging, ear flattening, varying the gaze, dipping high or low in air or water.

We can't fly, can't wag our tails, can't dance in the waters. We cannot, most of us, wreath our bodies seven times around with elegant quickness, like Christopher Smart's cat praising God. What we *can* do is *talk*. So talk. Or grunt, meow, caw, sing. This is part of what Hearne's trainers do: they rejoin the animals' expressive world. Take up the animals' sounds. When you walk out the door and the crows start up their chorus—talk back. When you return and the cats say hello (you know very well that they do)—answer. Say hello back.

Then there is the question of names. Even our veterinarian sends us home with the cats' names in scare quotes. As if we give them names (personality, individuality, a place in our social relations) only out of indulgence, or soft-headedness. Still not "real" names. But they *are* individuals, they do have a place in our social relations. Their names are as real as our own. Ecofeminist Carol Adams's description of a genuine companion animal immediately rings true: "When we watch someone who has a companion animal interact with that animal, we see in that relationship a recognition of that animal's individuality, or, in a sense, that animal's personhood: given a name, touched and caressed, a life that interacts with and informs another's."[2] The last phrase is exact. A name, touch, and "a life that interacts with and informs another's:" these things go together, perhaps even necessarily.

So call animals by name. Acknowledge in that way their place in community with us. Look carefully enough to have the right to give and use those names. Jane Goodall's editors, remember, initially refused to publish her papers on the great apes because she used names for the animals rather than numbering them. Yet what the names reflect, her insistence on treating the animals personally—as individuals, with whom she had individual relationships—was crucial to her success. Individual names, faces, personalities, histories:

> Jane recognized their faces, some of which were as dear to her as her own family's: Mr McGregor; scheming, round-faced Mike; David Greybeard, whose eyes she considered the most beautiful she had ever seen; ancient, wrinkled Mr Worzle. The females were equally recognizable. . . . [But] when Jane first arrived, three years earlier, all the chimps had simply looked like black spots in her borrowed binoculars, a thousand yards away.[3]

Here the act of naming, of finding the name, and following through on the connections that using a name implies, were essential. Animals are not going to use our names (though some chimps did to the point of actually saying "Mama" and "Papa" for their adoptive human parents),[4] but, as Adams suggests, they certainly show their attentiveness in other ways, "interacting with and informing" us as well in all the ways that I have tried to suggest in earlier chapters. Naming is one of *our* ways.

Historian Keith Thomas traces the history, in England, of what we might call "semi-names" for animals: stereotyped names or categories of names for certain species, like cows named for flowers, Marigiold or Lily, or fond descriptive names, like Gentle, Button, Proudlook. Horse names have their own equally dense history. Dogs got short names, easy to call out, descriptive or hortatory, often epithets or occupations. Peter Beckford's 1781 book *Thoughts on Hunting,* reflecting the tradition of naming all the foxhounds in a litter with names beginning with the name initial, lists, under "E," for example, Eager, Earnest, Effort, Elegant, Envoy.[5] Even today's suburban cats and dogs seem to have more varied and more expressive names than humans tend to get. All of this reminds us that animal naming, carefully or even not so carefully practiced, is not just an extension of human naming. Like human naming, it affirms and cements relationship; but the names are also kept carefully distinct. This is a *mixed* community—the names reflect its varied textures.

Yet another matter of naming is the use of personal pronouns, "he" or "she" rather than "it," to speak of nonhuman creatures. This too, remember, Goodall's editors initially refused to allow. But this too is only a matter of proper acknowledgment. They *are* gendered beings—even if spayed, though spaying *changes* their genderedness—and certainly they are *live* beings rather than mere objects. We know that animals are being systematically reduced to mere objects on a massive scale all around us, and there are many ways in which this reduction must be resisted. To refuse the dishonesty of that little word "it" is at least a beginning, an insistence on truth that keeps open an awareness that we are speaking of genuine creatures in their own rights. Psychologist Carol Cina argues that the "metamessage" of "it" is that the animal (she is speaking specifically of an insect) is, for one thing,

> decisively not like me, for I have gender and I am alive. The metamessage says that we are qualitatively different. [S]tep one in the justification of the domination hierarchy. Since an "it" also has

the character of an object rather than a living being, we are impelled . . . to impute moral superiority to that which is alive. We then tumble into an intellectual and emotional . . . justification for control over the insect. No need to treat the insect as an agency of consequence in the biosphere.[6]

"He" or "she" asserts commonality rather than difference, life rather than objecthood, "an agency of consequence in the biosphere." With my daughter, the use of "he" or "she" always leads to more questions, questions springing from a sense of identification, from the intrigue she seems to feel with all living things. "What is she [the ladybug, the bee] doing?" "Why does she like to fly around?" New schemas. The dismissal, and the death-dealing, are stayed.

Much more could be said about naming. Anthropologist Calvin Martin, citing native practices around the world, warns us not to use animal names for other things, for manufactured, human things—cars, battleships, missiles.[7] A falcon is *not* like a fighter plane or a car: we get both the falcon and the products wrong if we equate them, and the hint of magic, of power, of thrill in making the equation is precisely what is dangerous about it. Animals do have powers, and naming (or not naming) is a response to those powers. "For hunter societies, words of animal and plant, words of place, and the enabling powers of one's earth-derived artifice were transmitted by these beings themselves. It was essential to continue observing this manner of speech and artifice if one hoped to maintain a truthful and harmonious relationship to one's habitat."[8]

But naming, and even language as a whole, are still only a small part of the landscape of acknowledgment. Vicki Hearne, in the story with which this chapter began, puts more emphasis on the *body*. "Body language." She speaks, remember, of a "way of moving [that] fits into the spaces shaped by the animals' awareness." It is by their bodies, from their ways of moving, that she can tell the trainers from the actors and the academics. They acknowledge the other creatures bodily—or do not. The trainers turn toward the animals, move aside, mold their movements to the animals. None of this is a mystery. We know what it means when others turn toward us or turn away in a conversation, walk right through us or walk around. With other animals, the same actions mean exactly the same things.

We look—or don't. There may be "eye contact" (at any rate with animals who *have* eyes). What then? Even between ourselves, we can refuse the reciprocity that returning the look, that letting it "bounce," implies. With each other we know very well that there is a difference between the objectifying stare and the look that interacts, that acknowledges the presence of someone else. You can look at me too like a piece of furniture. For the existential philosopher Jean-Paul Sartre, the objectifying stare is the look that turns the one looked at into a *thing:* that pigeonholes, exhausts, and discards you in the same instant. Other animals know that stare very well too. Evernden, remember, following Lopez, argues that objectification and the resistance to objectification are part of the "conversation of death" between predator and prey. Hearne, speaking of how academics look at animals, writes of "the stare that makes almost all animals uneasy." Animals resist it. Direct looks from strangers elicit immediate aggression in wolves and gorillas, immediate evasion in cats. The tourist camera evokes anger in you and me, a more lethal response from bears.

Those are the failures. Success is more fleeting, also more unsettling. "The closest we come to actually touching the interior of another animal," writes minster and activist Gary Kowalski, "is through the eyes."[9] At any rate that is one experience: "eye contact" is a kind of opening to the soul. More often, though, it seems that the one really "touched" by eye contact is oneself.

Looking into another person's eyes, I fall in upon myself, I become aware of myself, aware of myself being seen. So, too, in eye contact with another animal. I feel *myself* "touched." I am aware of being focused on, if nothing else. So simple a thing as binocular vision may actually be crucial for this kind of acknowledgment or connection. In any case, I may, for instance, recognize the wariness in the eyes of an animal looking at me, and so recognize the character of my own presence to the animal, for better or worse, and hence the perhaps-strange character of my own look. D. H. Lawrence, in "A Doe at Evening":

> . . . I looked at her
> And felt her watching;
> I became a strange being . . ."[10]

I become strange; I become aware of myself, I might come to question my own comportment, I at any rate recognize that I *have* a comportment toward the other creature. I am no longer alone.

We touch—or don't. Touch is crucial: another avenue to, or rather form of, the soul. Goodall writes of the first moment of contact with a chimpanzee: "At that moment there was no need of any scientific knowledge to understand his reassurance. The soft pressure of his fingers spoke to me not through my intellect but through a more primitive emotional channel: the barrier of untold centuries which has grown up during the separate evolution of man and chimpanzee was, for those few seconds, broken down.[11] Wilhelm Reich spoke of "body armor": rigidity of posture, tightness, the refusal to touch or to be touched, unwillingness to move aside or shape your movements to the movements of others. We may shrink, involuntarily, from each other's touch, or from an animal's: or tighten up. Conversely, we may welcome touch and reach out ourselves. The point is, all of this *shows*. The body reveals much more than we think. Hearne claims to be able to tell handlers from academics at two hundred paces. It cannot be exactly subtle—not to any creature who looks. Even when subtle to us, of course, bodily signs are the signs that other animals, like our own children, read first, and exquisitely better than we do. This is why it is perfectly possible for people to believe that other animals are ethically "considerable" (or at least to believe that they believe it), and even to want to establish some kind of relationship, and yet to fail utterly to do so. (Also vice versa.) The body answers for us. Learning to answer differently, learning the "letting go" of genuinely touching and being touched, takes time. It is a matter of habit: more like a kind of posture than a kind of belief.

I want now to try to say what acknowledgment at its core *is;* what all the examples so far offered are examples *of.*

Naming, meeting the look, touching and being touched: all of these are ways of establishing, affirming, and maintaining social relations. Not magic; but a genuinely different kind of behavior and a different kind of attention. Mary Midgley: "People who succeed well with [such animals as cats, horses, and camels] do not do so just by some abstract, magical human superiority, but by interacting socially with them—by attending to them and coming to understand how various things appear from each animal's point of view."[12] *By interacting socially with them!* What "connection" with other animals ultimately requires is a set of practices and comportments that invites connection, that approaches them as co-inhabitants of a shared world from the start; by taking them seriously as creatures who *have* a point of view, and by, in Midgley's exactly chosen word, "attending": by both paying attention and showing it.

Something very personal and demanding is asked of us. Listen to the language that emerges among certain writers who do "succeed with animals" or who are close to those who do. Grizzly tracker Doug Peacock insists on what he calls "interspecific tact." Wendell Berry speaks of an "etiquette" of nature. Calvin

Martin, just mentioned, citing a global range of native practices, speaks of "courtesy." Poet Gary Snyder writes of "grace." Philosopher Tom Birch writes of "generosity of spirit" and "considerateness." All of these terms have their home in a discourse of manners and personal bearing. We are speaking of a kind of gracefulness or circumspection: of something very close to us, bound up with who we are and how we immediately bear ourselves toward others and in the world. The issue is one of comportment; or, to adopt that suggestive term of both Berry's and Snyder's, *etiquette.*

This is not quite what one expects to be asked at the present point in the contemporary discussion of animals. What we are usually offered as the necessary step beyond the familiar exploitation and dismissal is something much more formal and moralistic: animal *ethics.* Most people now have heard of the idea of "animal rights," though not all philosophers who wish to take other animals seriously actually attribute them rights, strictly speaking; the other main view extends the great welfare principles to include most other animals.[13] In any event, we do not expect to be asked for a kind of response that is much more personal and open-ended, and that lives in what we may well consider the quite secondary realm of "manners." Yet that, after all, may be what we need.

The philosophers who have opened the ethical questions are to be honored for prying open a dark door in the peculiar philosophical universe, as well as for their immense contribution toward ending the grossest kinds of "reduction" of animals in factory farms and product labs. It is certainly *a* necessary step. It may well be that their aim was only to take this step, not to give a complete and conclusive answer to the question how humans ought to relate to other animals, although that sometimes is how they are now read. In any case, it turns out that we need a kind of guidance that these ethical theories do not give. We need guidance about *relationship*. Animal welfare views do not help: their issue is pain, usually of the most gross and obvious kind, and (officially at least) pains are to be added up, looked at collectively rather than individually, and weighed against whatever gains, even for other species, they might offer. That even the grossest impositions are always wrong is not a given.[14] Animal rights theories initially seem more promising: the associated language of respect does seem to bear on relational style. But, in the end, not in the necessary way. Rights serve to protect and insulate us from each other, to distance us, they are adversarial in nature; whereas we are talking about establishing *connections*. Less distance, not more; less insulation, more interaction.

Peter Singer, foremost of the animal welfare theorists, points out that respecting other animals is a very different matter from sentimentalizing them.[15] Though a kind of sentimentalism about animals has its points—Chapter 5 suggests that sometimes it may be our only way of holding on to a sense of what they could be—it also tends, in the actual practice of relationship, to patronize them in ways that undercut acknowledgment. Singer so far is surely right. But it doesn't follow that we can go on without any actual practice of relationship at all. Singer declares that, apart from righting the ethical wrongs done to other animals, he is not particularly interested in other animals.[16] Perhaps for this very reason, he himself in the end patronizes them too: analogizing them to retarded humans, for example, in order to argue that their pains are no less significant for being different than ours. Genuine difference—and the immense range of advanced possibilities that in fact can be opened up by and with a whole range of other creatures (with the retarded, too, for that matter, who are not at all merely depressed-capacity versions of "normality")— never emerge at all.

Transhuman etiquette? What could such a thing actually mean?

Wolfgang Kohler, testing chimpanzees' capacities to use tools, hung a clump of bananas from the ceiling, out of reach, and then left sticks and boxes in the room to see if the chimps would use them as tools to knock down the fruit or to step up to it. Sometimes they did; this was regarded as a great triumph for chimp intelligence. Kohler then moved the sticks and boxes out of sight, to test whether the animals could think of the sticks and go to find them when the connection was not immediate. Sometimes—less often—they did. Another triumph.

Most of us know this story. Cartoonist Gary Larson memorialized it in a cartoon showing a (human) cleaning person reaching vainly for the bananas, ignoring the broom she holds in her other hand. But it is a strange business, actually, once we think about it. As Midgley remarks about this case:

> Tool use . . . is rather alien to a chimp's natural *interests*. His problems are not usually physical, but social, and his attention in a difficulty goes at once to a social solution. Thus, Kohler remarked that he had trouble keeping his apes to the task of getting the suspended bananas themselves, since their first idea in this predicament was to lead him to them and ask him to lift them down. Other experimenters sometimes report the same sort of thing as an embarrassment to their work. But as "experimenting" is a notion nobody has explained to the chimps, what they do here is by no means stupid, and they might well think of the unresponsive humans as stupid or mulish.[17]

The chimps seem to have thought that they had some sort of relationship with Kohler and his assistants, within which the most intelligent and socially sensitive thing to do is precisely to ask them to lower the bananas. In fact, the chimps were right. They responded sensibly and trustingly in a social setting, and *that*, arguably, was the real triumph. But that affirmation of commonality, of friendship, of everyday comradeship with members of another species who in general treat them with friendship—that is also precisely what humans, even these seemingly most scientific and even sympathetic humans, were unprepared or unwilling to recognize. It only "embarrassed" them. They could not see that it actually represented a much more marvelous capacity of the animal than the one they were investigating.

Human insensitivity to social setting and sheer doggedness in the wrong direction is nicely illustrated by a story from Goodall's research station in which the roles are reversed.

Once Geza Teleki [one of Goodall's co-workers at the time] . . . had followed the chimps down into the valley and around noon discovered that he had forgotten to bring his lunch. The chimps were feeding on fruit in the trees at the time, and he decided to try to knock some fruit from nearby vines with a stick. For about ten minutes he leaped and swatted with his stick but didn't manage to knock down any fruit. Finally an adolescent named Sniff collected a handful of fruit, came down the tree, and dropped the fruit into Geza's hands.[18]

Teleki could have asked the chimps to get the bananas for him. This occurred immediately to them, in the parallel situation, although the experimenters in that case only found it embarrassing. But it never occurs to Teleki. The chimps have to treat him as a charity case. He is rescued in the end by an adolescent, no less.

The possibility of human social clumsiness in such cases is not even imagined. But the flaw is a very general one. Most animal researchers take themselves to be entitled, in fact obliged, to approach other animals as some kind of "question." But this very approach, ultimately, represents our refusal of a social relation with them. This is what Teleki and Kohler lack—as sympathetic, "nice," or otherwise benign as they no doubt are. What they lack is any serious attention to the chimps' own point of view: any serious attention to how the world, in particular their relationships to the researchers, actually seems to the animals. We have looked at some other, more egregious examples, such as Jim Nollman's account of the researchers who shot howler monkeys out of the trees in order to radio-band them and study, of all things, their sociability. In all these cases it is precisely a social point of view that is lacking.

Put animals in question in the most profound way possible; ask "Is there anyone in there?"; wonder whether they are capable of any communication at all; pretend that we know nothing at all about them and have no relationship with them—and they will be reduced to questionable beings. Humans, put in the position of these test subjects, would fail too, in exactly the same way and for exactly the same reasons. If I want to find out how well *you* can use tools or how well you can talk, I don't do "research" to find out. I ask you to change the tire, or strike up a conversation. Of course we test each other all the time: we interview each other for jobs, tease, flirt, try to get some information we need or find out whether we can trust the teacher, and so on and on. But in doing all this we do not begin from a position of skepticism about whether there is anything going on on the other side at all. *That* we assume: you are not some kind of robot or refrigerator or space alien, but a being like me, a "subject" with my own point of view, some kind of will, some kind of depth. That assumption gives life to everything that follows: that is the essentially social move. But it is still an "assumption," logically; a piece of etiquette, even; what we might call, paralleling Chapter 5's talk of "self-validating reduction," something like "self-validating inclusion" or "self-validating *invitation*." We are seeking what we want to know within a context where relationship is already assumed and invited, and for that very reason something relational is more likely to be discovered, to develop.

Species lines do not affect this logic at all. Think of human relationships. To trust someone who is unsure of her own trustworthiness is a way to make her feel more trustworthy, and hence make it possible for her to become more trustworthy—just as pervasive mistrust tends to corrode trustworthiness. We have to *offer* trust: that is the "invitation." We invite others to deserve it. Parents' love creates a kind of safety and support that makes the blossoming of a child possible, just as the lack of that love becomes its own self-fulfilling disaster. When adults fall in love, each responds, in part, to a vision of the loved one's possibilities, possibilities that (perhaps) no one else could see who was not a lover; and it also helps to bring those possibilities into actuality. In just the same way, the howler monkeys, tranquilized and radio-tagged and reduced to shadowy movements on scientists' graphs, became companions, co-musicians, when Nollman invited them to join him playing the flute beneath their trees. Nollman had to go out on that limb first (almost literally, in this instance). Without creating such spaces, without seeking out ways in which we might connect with other animals, rather than "testing" them to see if they can "communicate," we will have no idea what other animals are actually capable of.

We now can ask what etiquette, so understood, might require—concretely. A first step would be to explore what kinds of tasks might actually constitute "intelligence" or "communication" *for other animals,* or rather, for specific species and populations of other animals, since other animals vary tremendously. Tool use, as Midgley notes, is actually alien to chimps' natural interests. Even the terms of the famous language-use experiments are wholly human. First the attempt was made to teach chimps spoken human language; then, after a decade or so, researchers concluded that the chimps just don't have the right vocal cords for humanlike speech; the project shifted to the manipulation of symbols, or sign language.[19] That symbolic language should be particularly important to chimps (or to most animals), however, is not at all clear. Meanwhile, even certain self-styled radical thinkers, rejecting the scientific skepticism we have been discussing, still imagine that more-than-human dialogues will look just like human dialogues. The stream or the anthill is supposed to speak to us literally as do you and I.[20] But this is surely no more promising: it ignores the enormous differences between humans and the rest of the world just as totally and as enthusiastically as do the scientists. Either way, we are still approaching other animals congratulating ourselves on our own enlightenment, but actually receptive, at best, to only a few very particular and very anthropomorphic responses. If "taking the social view" means looking at things *their* way, we must ask how it is that *they* might choose to "connect"—and when they might choose to connect, and where, and why.

Take, for example, "communication." Suppose that we simply ask what modes of exchange are truly shared between humans and particular other animals. Truly shared: this is not an invitation to pick modes of exchange that are centrally part of *our* practices and at best glancingly or laboriously taken up by others (perhaps even other human cultures). Think, for instance, of very old systems of shared signs: native hunting cultures, for one, in which humans hunt in just the ways and for just the same prey as certain nonhuman predators, like the Inuit and the polar bears hunting seals—when Inuit and bear are not hunting each other. Here the shared world was never abandoned in the first place. (Barry Lopez reports that the Inuit find biologists' ways of studying animals, as "questions" to be answered by observations leading to generalizations, absolutely unfathomable.)[21] The animals are more like relatives—in totemic cultures as well as from the evolutionary point of view, they *are* relatives—and invite a fond or exasperated but always engaged and open-ended relationship, even, so the claim goes, when being hunted.

Still, I shall concentrate here on the possibilities for us moderns, cut off as we surely are from most of the old shared sign systems. You and I cannot share a world of signs with the polar bear in the way that Inuit hunters might. But it turns out that we may have hopes every bit as wild; only the exemplars for us will be rather wildly different. Nollman, for one, has made a career of trying to find media of communication between species that do not force conversation into human terms from the start. He has tried to find media that create a kind of shared space with other creatures. Usually, too, he goes to them, in the wild, inviting but never forcing their participation. In his work, these are chiefly musical forms, like rhythm and melody, with which he has approached whales and dolphins (and a wide range of other creatures): as co-makers of music, in their own medium, and in the wild.[22]

Part of the inspiration came from listening to recordings of whale songs. Nollman asked himself whether there weren't human forms that more closely corresponded to whales' own vocalization patterns than the speech we are used to. The answer was clearly yes: jazz, for one thing. A range of other considerations back up this line of thought. Physiology, for one. Ecologist Sterling Bunnell:

> Eyesight in humans is a space-oriented distance-sight, which gives us complex simultaneous information in the form of analogic pictures but has poor time discrimination. Our auditory sense, however, has poor space perception but good time discrimination. Human languages are therefore comprised of fairly simple sounds arranged in elaborate temporal sequences. The cetacean audiory system is predominantly spatial, like our eyesight, with much simultaneous information and poor time resolution. So dolphin language apparently consists of extremely complex sounds which are perceived as a unit. A whole paragraph's information might be conveyed in one elaborate instantaneous heiroglyph. . . . It is not surprising, then, that captive dolphins at first seem more interested in music than in the human voice.[23]

Cetologist Paul Spong argues that music may be cetaceans' permanent preference, the responsiveness of captive orcas, for instance, to human sounds other than music being a product of the monotony of captivity and the acoustic deprivation of their concrete tanks.[24] Spong, like Nollman, writes of interactions with orcas, paddling among them in canoes and kayaks, greeting them, and finally also moving into music, flute-playing and synthesizer renditions of their own calls, imperfect but recognizable imitations that the orcas then imitated themselves.[25]

Nollman's own accounts are astonishing and moving, and, like the story of any true dialogue, take some time to tell. I reproduce just one, even this one abbreviated.

I pull out an electric guitar and pick out an arpeggiated D-major chord. . . . Then I switch to a G chord and play the same riff a fourth step higher. Then it's back to D for a while, up to A, and finally back to D again.

I played that same progression through an underwater sound system . . . for three nights in a row. All three nights the music attracted orcas. When I started playing, the whales could not be heard. After ten minutes of playing, the orcas began vocalizing, but from several miles away. Fifteen minutes later they arrived at the cove, and spent the next three hours interacting with the guitar music.

On the first night it seemed as if the whales vocalized constantly, not at all coordinated with the harmonic and rhythmical structure of the chord progression. On the second night, the whales arrived as I was getting my equipment ready to begin. One individual whale stepped out to take a kind of lead voice with the guitar playing. The rest of the pod chose to stay in the background, jibber-jabbering among themselves in a quieter tone which seemed unrelated to the unfolding ensemble playing at center stage. At the same time that the whales split into singer and Greek chorus, a group of humans appeared at the seaside sound studio. . . . They, too, began to comment among themselves at key places in the interaction. Sometimes the human observers would comment at the same moment that the observing orcas seemed also to comment. Once, the correlation was so clear that I had to stop playing a moment, just to get my bearings. . . .

The third night evolved into pure magic. . . . I began . . . by mimicking the standard stereotypical vocalization of the pod: a three-note frequency-modulated phrase that begins and ends on the D note. But this pattern is never frozen. Rather it varies in form by the addition or deletion of the speed of the glissando, by the fluidity of the legato. In other words, the whales' own language varies just exactly the same way that a jazz musician varies a standardized melody. And the whales seemed very aware of my own attempts to vary their own song by ending each of my phrases with a solid obbligato amen of D to C to E to D.

Unfortunately, the highest note available to my electric guitar is a mere C-sharp, an impenetrable half-step universe below the orcas' tonic note. Thus, in order to reach their register, I needed to bend the high string—something ordinarily not that difficult—but, in fact, rather clumsy to achieve hunched up in the dark fog while fingering up at the very top of the guitar neck. The first time I attempted the bend, the result sounded like a very respectable approximation of the orcas' own phrasing. . . . [I] repeated the phrase a second time. Suddenly, the high E string snapped. While I sat there in the thick night air fumbling through my guitar case for a fresh string, the orcas stepped up the intensity of their vocalizations. Calling, calling for me to rejoin the music. Every so often one of them would punctuate a long sinuous phrase with the obbligato.

I tightened up on the E string, and stubbornly plucked out the orcas' obbligato, but this time in C-sharp instead of D. The center-stage orca immediately answered by repeating the phrase in C-sharp. Otherwise, it was the exact same melody. From that point on, the dialogue between us centered around the common C-sharp chromatic scale. And the conversation continued for more than another hour in very similar fashion. . . . What the orca and the guitar player settled upon was the conversational form of dialogue. Each of us waited until the other had finished vocalizing before the other one started. In order for such a form to work properly, both of us had to become acutely conscious of each other's beginnings and endings. Once and a while, one of us would inadvertently step out before the other one had completed his piece, but in general, the form of the dialogue was clearly working. And as such, the resultant musical exchange never digressed to a mere call and response. . . . There was always a feeling of care and of sensitivity, of conscious musical evolution within the time frame of a single evening's music. I might play three notes and the orca might repeat the same progression back to me, but with two or three new notes added on the end. Once, I made an error in my repetition of one of the orca's phrases. The whale repeated the phrase back again—but this time at half the speed!

After an hour of this intense concentration . . . there was nothing else to do, no place else to go with the dialogue but directly into the sharply etched reggae rhythm of the previous two nights. I played it, inexplicably, in the key of A. The orca immediately responded with a short arpeggio of the A chord. When I hit the D triad on the fifth downbeat, the orca vocalized a G note, also right on the fifth downbeat. It was the suspended note of the D triad. Then back to A and the orca responded in A, again on the downbeat. The agile precision of rhythm, pitch, and harmony continued through the entire twelve-bar verse.[26]

There is much more in this vein, and tapes to match, but it is the spirit of this encounter that counts for us.

Utilizing the language of my own musical training, it feels very comfortable to name such an encounter a jam session. . . . But perhaps I stand guilty of bald-faced anthropomorphosing [sic]. In other words, for [the orcas'] signature whistles to be called music, must not the orca hold a concept that is at least analogous to what we humans know as music? I disagree. What we invented was neither human nor orca. Rather, it was *interspecies* music. A co-created original.[27]

Much of this work, of course, remains sketchy and scientifically marginal. Precisely its sociability, its willingness to relate to other creatures as, as it were, social equals, makes it irredeemably suspicious to the hardheads. Still, in fact, it is only by actually joining other animals in their own worlds, and trying to discover shared terms—to strike up what Donna Haraway calls "non-innocent conversations"—that in the end we will learn anything very deep about what they are capable of, or rather what we are capable of together. Nollman is very clear about the need for etiquette, especially what I have called "self-validating invitation." "Meeting the animal halfway," he insists, is a *precondition* of communication:

> Like any music, interspecies music communicates the energy exchange of harmony. Like any successful harmony, it is sustained as long as the participants co-create in the here and now. What this implies in actual practice is that the human must first acknowledge the other being as his or her equal. In many cases the human must actually sit with the animal as a student sits with a teacher. And it is at this point of recognition, when we truly meet the animal halfway, that the relationship finally emerges.[28]

The acknowledgment of the other comes *first.* It does not follow upon the other being's ability to prove himself or herself, it is not a reward or a kind of good grade on a test. In fact, we are as much at stake as the other creature. It is not as though we are really in the privileged position of being entitled to administer such tests; the challenge is to see if we—we and the other animal or animals—can work out something together. And if so, then we are, in Nollman's words, "sucked into . . . an operative and very complex . . . communication network." It does not follow that we then know what the orca feel, that we have somehow merged with them—any more than we might just merge with each other. Maybe it sometimes happens, but that is the special case. "To the contrary: the key to a continuing communication relationship with orca, or with any animal for that matter, is [to b]ecome a patient and creative conversationalist."[29] That is the cocreation, "jamming" together. Not merging but dialogue.

None of this stops with whales, or with music. Across all the species and across every expressive medium we might imagine similar possibilities. Take the most sharply different species we might imagine: say, seagulls. Just as with orcas, we have to ask *not* something like "How could we get seagulls (say) to talk?"—it's not our place to "get" them to talk!—but again, as Nollman asks: what media do we share with these animals in a way that might be developed into a more expressive means of interaction? Nollman raises this very question. He suggests *flying* with seagulls: hang-gliding, for example. "Perhaps a seagull 'speaks' through a subtle variation in its flight patterns. . . . It may greet other seagulls differently than it greets an albatross or a piece of kelp, or a kelp forest."[30]

With birds, moreover, why not some sustained exchange of song? The species may be wildly different, but this medium, at least, is not. We know that birds, like dolphins, are profoundly responsive to music and learn their own "songs" and other birdsongs and melodies through experience. Well, birds are too mechanical, the skeptic says: they can only repeat themselves. Maybe, but how do we know? (How especially does the skeptic know? Skepticism is usually an excuse for not listening: another self-validating reduction.) Mockingbirds, the true masters, may learn up to two hundred different songs, and have been known to reproduce the sounds of train whistles, automobile horns, and barking dogs.[31] In my own neighborhood the owls duet with car alarms. I suppose they therefore think humans (or maybe just cars?) profoundly unintelligent, since we (or cars) are apparently so incapable of altering our sounds in the least to respond to *them*. ("Humans are too mechanical. . . .") Years ago, camping out with my stereo on a summer construction site, discovering classical music, I would play Handel long into the night, and even the little bats hanging on the walls of my lean-to throbbed and squeaked along to the "Hallelujah Chorus."

Just watch the winged beings, and listen. All of us might readily attend to the bluejay's calls in the backyard just as we would the calls of a dog or our neighbor. Climbing in the hills or walking in rolling country, you learn quickly to watch for unusual circling or gathering over the next hill. The birds tell us things we wouldn't otherwise know: something has died, something threatens, something has happened over there. In this way we begin to recognize a kind of sensory *co-presence* in the land, even when the senses involved are the same as ours but are in relation, at the moment, to some other part of the land. As I drive the freeway, I see the hawks perched on the high-tension wires at particular spots, or circling along with the turkey vultures overhead. Even here there is a sense of an animate presence beyond the human that broadens and deepens the human world. And correspondingly *they* watch *us*. Condors, for instance, are curious birds, as most scavengers are: they like watching us, apparently, which actually is one cause of their high mortality rate.[32]

There are expressive worlds centering on the body. An alligator scientist jumps in the alligator pond (with a stick): "I was pretty sure the alligators were communicating with subtle visual signals. Slight changes in body posture and body elevation in the water— things like that. But being on this boardwalk looking down on them, I wasn't able to see those slight changes very well. I thought that if I got at an alligator's eye level, it would be pretty easy for me at least to see what's relevant to an alligator."[33] A wonderful image. *Looking down* on the animals, he couldn't begin to understand them. Joining them, he could—or could, at least, "see what's relevant to an alligator." That, in this case, is what "interacting socially" required. It also turns out that alligators, as well as other "armored" animals such as turtles, are extremely sensitive to touch—odd as it may seem. In fact, alligator courtship is mostly a matter of, literally, "necking."[34] Who knows, perhaps the subtle touch will turn out to be one of the best means of human–reptile "contact," and the best human communicators will not be the scientists back on the boardwalk, and not even musicians fresh from jamming with whales, but those humans who specialize in *touch:* masseuses, maybe, or chiropractors, or practitioners of the Alexander technique.

Elephants, chimps, monkeys draw and paint.[35] Might we not find ways to communicate with them through pictures? Or, say, through computer-aided graphic design? Cartooning? Entire esoteric arts are based on just watching animals *move.* Tai Chi evolved out of careful attention to animals' ways of fighting: a snake, finally injuring and driving off a hawk, lent its flexible and softer tactics to human fighters. Even some of the movements are named after other life forms: one stands, for example, "like a tree" (not at all rigid!). So here the best human communicators with certain animals might turn out to be Aikido masters or ballet dancers or Hopi Indians, who already dance with rattlesnakes.[36]

Or high divers, mail carriers, photographers, babies. Acrobats, parachute jumpers, meteorologists, parents, waitresses. Just plain people. Maybe even philosophers. Almost anything is possible. But almost nothing is possible until we venture to try, as equals, in the very particular sense of "etiquette." Meeting the animal, as Nollman says, halfway.

8

Is It Too Late?

I admit to bouts of despair. Driving home, too long, on the freeway, watching the red-tails disconsolately spiral into the jet-trailing sunsets, knowing that even this degree of nostalgia is foreign to most of the other drivers. Holding my daughter in my arms, watching the storms sweep across the piedmont, trying to show her—what? The little fragments of sky and clouds that we can see through the buildings, beyond the streetlights and power lines? Malls everywhere, McDonald's Playlands, to the point that they finally form our children's very idea of play, practically their idea of life itself. So many fabulous creatures gone or teetering on the brink of extinction. Self-validating reductions of the rest, nothing to be done about them, now enthusiastically carried to the extremes that will probably be my children's normality, like the genetic engineers' pursuit of the headless chicken. "Nature" now imaginable to most of us, thanks to the newspapers, mainly as the site of expensive vacations somewhere else—and once again everything conspires to make it so, since the places where most of us live are so relentlessly and completely "developed." Noise and light everywhere; now the utterly unbelievable and yet all-too-serious proposal for orbiting advertisements, satellite Coke logos now to serve as our own twice-as-bright and ten-times-as-fast moons.[1]

No solace, it seems, anywhere, not even in the stars. The difference between what this world is becoming and what it was and still could be is so overwhelming that no one can face it all the time.

And yet, in a certain sense, at the very same time, the more-than-human remains, all around us, and will remain as long as we live on this planet at all, or live anywhere. Every moment, all around us, the air still stirs, our cousins the fungi grow, and the very rocks move. A daddy longlegs periodically takes up residence in my car, rides back and forth with me to work. I see one of his legs sticking out from underneath the glove compartment as I drive, and I am comforted already. Computers have "bugs" worldwide, and the original "bug" was, of course, a bug: a beetle or something that shorted out the first UNIVAC. The proverbial grass cracks all pavements. Last spring, after a camping trip with friends in Northern Michigan, we watched an all-night electrical storm, for hours scintillating the sky almost constantly, and torrential rains. The next day's newspapers say that Chicago had its heaviest rains in thirty years. Freeway underpasses are flooded. Tonight, too, the air is crackly; how we love the weather, even now, perhaps especially now! We still live *in* this planet, not on it—still linked to its waters and winds by the very rhythms of our bodies, still electrified by it, still bugged by it—and always will.

Our identifications, our totems, are still animal, earthy; and they are all still there. Driving to work I pass the school buses: the "Eagles" from Lafayette Elementary, the Triton High School "Hawks," the Dunn Public School "Greenwaves." The teams from my southern Wisconsin high school (in a town called Spring Green, a school district called River Valley) were the "Blackhawks"; the name goes back to the Sauk war chief Black Hawk—not that in high school we were ever told this—whose rebellion led him through those parts in 1837. Spring Green, just downriver from Sauk City, the fertile riverbank that was the Sauks' city. The real Sauk ended up in Kansas; the first white settlers in Wisconsin came to be called "badgers"—subsequently the University of Wisconsin totem animal—after their style of winter squatting on Sauk land, burrowed into the ground imitating the real badgers. The Sauk lived in houses. All of this, though, is a long story, or rather many stories.[2] The point is only that *every* place, actually, has this kind of depth, this kind of "thick ecology," natural and historical, fabulous and horrible; and, like the depth of my own youth-place, it is closer to the surface than we imagine, memorialized for example in the names we now use without thinking. Or draining through the dozens of creeks that make up my old river valley, every time it rains.

No: this Earth is not lost, cannot be lost. Even the astronauts take it—metal, air, water, fire, and each other—with them when they go. We can forget it, maybe, but it will not forget us.

What can we *do?* we ask. But there is everything to do. Watch the spiders. Watch the skies. Walk. Garden. Let the lawn go wild. Feed the birds. Learn the birds. Seek out the stories of your place, pay attention to the names. Talk to the animals, talk about animals without that little pronoun "it." Pay attention. Arriving one evening on a cold and windy ocean beach, we see some sort of sand figure in the distance—not one of the innumerable sand castles. We go down to look. Someone has made a sand porpoise, perfectly proportioned, brushed sand. We walk along the beach, our two year old dancing in the light surf. Sit by the sand figure. Ten minutes later, porpoises are playing offshore. Spouting, diving, following the offshore sandbars as the tide changes. The Earth is alive; there is magic everywhere.

Stop the destruction: that is the community and political imperative. Systematic recycling is crucial; so is pollution control, habitat protection, an end to factory farming, usable mass transit, sustainable agriculture, an enhanced Endangered Species Act, and on and on. These points are almost universally agreed upon in principle, however recalcitrant we may be in practice. It is far cheaper to conserve electricity—creating what Amory Lovins calls "negawatts"—than to build new generating capacity, especially when the ecological costs of electricity generation are factored in, but even if they are not.[3] It is far cheaper and more sensible to plan products so that recycling is easy—*"pre*cycling"—than to pay attention only after the things are made, after they have been designed and manufactured with no attention to anything but the manufacturer's ease and profits. Even economists agree.

Practice is what counts, though, someone will say. Is any of this actually practical? Take, say, quiet zones. Pie in the sky, one thinks. But regularly I hear of islands and valleys that are inhabited but have no cars: Mackinac Island in Michigan's Mackinac Straits, several islands off the Carolina coast, others I don't want to mention. Little by little, if you look, an entire alternative world begins to emerge beyond the world of the official "realism." Expensive vacationland, some of these places, to be sure—at least that is the only way the ad writers can understand them. Yet part of the expensiveness and desirability of such places is precisely their quiet. We recognize this, which is already half the battle. Why are they not emulated at home? Ah, but perhaps they are—quietly. Ask around. Some of my friends live in a cooperatively owned and managed development, the houses clumped around the periphery with shared open, natural, and quiet space at the center. New developments all over the country are being similarly designed. Urban creeks, buried underground or channeled straight and narrow, are coming back out of their confinement; there is now an entire organization called the National Coalition to Restore Urban Waters.[4] Restored wetlands are beginning to replace shopping centers.[5] My own neighborhood, built paralleling a small creek, just rezoned itself to preserve its trees and open space and modest style of building. The city ordinance allowing neighborhoods to undertake rezonings requires the neighborhood to identify itself in some natural, nongerrymandered way. We identify in effect by miniwatershed (a kind of minibioregionalism at work here!): our road twists and turns alongside a small creek. That main road, as I have said, is also a one-lane, small, slow road, a walker's road, and one of the key aims of the rezoning is an insistence on keeping it that way: small, and *quiet*.

Practicality? Organic foods, unheard of twenty years ago, are now common enough that conventional food producers, poor things, are complaining that people may actually "overreact" to the latest pesticide scare and switch. Vegetarianism, on the utter fringe twenty years ago, is now familiar enough that people feel they need excuses for eating meat. Twenty years ago, whales and dolphins were being slaughtered all over the oceans without a second thought; today the International Whaling Commission itself dances around total whaling bans. Twenty-five years ago, we didn't even have an Environmental Protection Agency; today it is a Cabinet-level department, its enabling legislation together with the Clean Air and Clean Water acts and the Endangered Species Act impose direct economic costs on the scale of $125 billion a year, and 75 percent of the U.S. population approves.[6] Now *that's* "practicality."

Besides, who says the world is practical? A five-hundred-year-old Hindu sect has been hugging trees and protecting wild animals for centuries; now the wild deer walk right up to them and listen to their conversations.[7] Are they practical? Were their tree-hugging martyrs, 250 years ago? Ten minutes from my urban home there is thick forest where eighty years ago farmland was eroded and abandoned. Succession into hardwoods is starting. Who would have dreamed it a century ago? Were the farmers practical? Were the reforesters? Now we have before us proposals to turn half of the Great Plains into "Buffalo Commons." Already throughout New England the wilderness trails cross old stone-wall farms, two hundred years ago. The face of the land may be again utterly transformed in another century.

Change is the order of the day. Think just of one device, the automobile, barely on the horizon only a century ago, now having spectacularly rearranged every aspect of our lives (their noise everywhere, roads everywhere, fifty thousand American highway deaths a year taken for granted) and the entire productive resources of the planet (assembly lines everywhere, oil rigs in deep ocean and Arctic tundra, carbon monoxide emissions transforming the entire atmosphere), almost none of it planned in advance by any kind of planning agency, one step just leading to the next. *Anything* is possible.

There is, finally, the question of fatalism. Yes, the world still trembles all around us. Yes, we can garden and recycle and learn the birds. Yes, change is the order of the day. Still, is there any point to it? Are we not doomed already? Every year my students are better-informed on environmental issues but less optimistic about doing anything. If global warming or ozone depletion or toxics-induced immunity-deficiency diseases do not do us in, they say, something else will. The Earth is past saving already.

I suppose that this could be true. Perhaps the jig is really up. Yet there is a strange and striking way in which this fatalism too freezes and fixes the Earth, just like the fantasies of control and benign management that environmentalism sets itself up against. Either to imagine that we can "save" the Earth or to imagine that the Earth is definitively past "saving" wildly overrates our own powers to intercede, to make a difference, and indeed just to know. The truth is that we barely know this place—how can we know enough to give up on it?

Almost all of our constructs, even the best theories, remain uncertain, more uncertain than we usually admit, particularly as the issues become more global, more dependent on projections, computer models, ecological theories, incomplete data. In the 1960s we were told, on the best of evidence, that a billion or more people would starve to death by 1990 because population had irrevocably outgrown food supplies. Since then, population growth has decelerated while food supplies have increased, and although widespread starvation and malnutrition exist, they are arguably results of political rather than Malthusian causes. Global warming is the disaster-forecast of choice so far in the 1990s, but the evidence is again far from clear. It is not clear that global temperatures are actually increasing; there are marginal increases, perhaps depressed by recent volcanic eruptions, perhaps exaggerated by "heat island effects." Most measuring stations are located near cities; global temperatures as measured from space are not increasing. It is not clear that the reported increase doesn't have other explanations. The determinants of Earth's temperature are almost incomprehensibly complicated: variations in solar activity and even small variations in the tilt of Earth's orbit are crucial; meanwhile, none of our theories explain the actual empirical phenomena, such as the marked lack of warming at the poles. It is not clear that global warming, if it really does happen, will raise the oceans. The Antarctic glacial shield was formed thirty million years ago and has withstood much warmer temperatures than are predicted at present. Since a warmer globe will experience more evaporation and precipitation, there will be more snow on the polar ice caps, thickening them: some recent estimates suggest that the sea may actually *drop*.[8] And so on and on the debates rage.

I do not mean that we may as well go on as we are going. Any rational policy under conditions of uncertainty aims to minimize risks. Rather than require proof that our present course is disastrous before we change it, we ought to require proof that it is *not* disastrous before we embark on it. Hidden dangers make caution all the more compelling, like "risk multipliers," processes that intensify other processes. Global warming may, for example, speed up the decomposition of the dead organic matter that now lies on forest floors, flooding the atmosphere with vast new quantities of carbon dioxide and accelerating further warming.[9] Also, equally obviously, a great many threats are not uncertain at all: the bulldozers down the street; Chernobyls-in-the-making all around the globe; the handfuls of captive California condors and free whooping cranes, last of their kinds, susceptible to any odd malady at any moment.

But a fundamental uncertainty remains: that is the point. This Earth eludes us. It eludes the pesticide makers, who find each new chemical shortly greeted by resistant insects that are even more destructive and harder to control. It eludes the nuclear industry's planners, unable to find any place, even deep within the earth, to entomb nuclear wastes, because even the rocks move. It eludes the paleontologists, who estimate that, even now, we have discovered at best 1 percent of dinosaur species[10]—who knows what awaits us, buried in the rocks? It eludes the computer modelers, who still, apparently, even now, have no idea where a billion tons of carbon dioxide—a seventh or more of the total dumped into the atmosphere from human sources—goes every year,[11] though some of them confidently go on to predict, or deny, global warming anyway. And this earth eludes our fatalism. Prediction is dangerous, as E. F. Schumacher once said, especially about the future.

The temptation is to take uncertainty as some kind of nuisance, or as a threat to the environmentalist agenda, as if belief in the environmental disaster scenario of the moment were some kind of litmus test of environmentalism. But the real point is that the future is *open*. We don't know where this Earth is going, any more than we know where it has been, or even where it is. Everything could be worse than we think, or better, but it will almost certainly be different than we think. All we can do is act on our best guesses and most fervent hopes.

Much is lost: unquestionably, achingly. But recognize this world as open-ended, wild, wily, and there is a kind of arched eyebrow even in our mourning. Rather than it now being "too late," it is *early*—in a deep sense, it will *always* be early. Our own possibilities are only barely explored; the possibilities of the "mixed community" and of wild connection and of the land even less so. We may yet learn to feel the air itself as a medium of connection with the whole Earth. Wholly unbelievable life forms may find their ways out of the rainforests, as some already have. (Who knows: an AIDS virus in reverse?) Or out of the oceans, like the coelacanth, believed extinct for seventy million years, redis-covered off South Africa in 1938, made into a cause célèbre by an eccentric British icthyologist—a story that sounds like something out of a Gary Larson cartoon, except that it is true.[12] Dinosaurs are not extinct either: it turns out they evolved into birds.[13] The littlest and flightiest from the biggest and the most plodding. Whales evolved from a doglike land mammal that came from the sea and then, a few hundred million years later, went back. And nothing could be stranger than what is already around us: fungi, flamingos, fundamentalists, elephants rumbling to each other across the savannas. Even our own "artificial" computer intelli-gence, if ever achievable, will inevitably stand on the side of the Other, the different—will demand *relationship*. What new coel-acanths must still swim below the waters we think we know so well! What old goddesses may reemerge, like Lovelock's Gaia, through some arcane measuring devices? The jig is up? Not likely.

We want to know "the answer?" There is no answer. No bumper-sticker slogans, no blueprints, no preformulated and decisive solutions to anything that can be specifically and easily formulated as "the" environmental crisis. We cannot "Save the Earth." So far from there being any guarantees, any stopping points, everything must be continuously rethought from the beginning. Even that notion of "the Earth," like "environment," is a snare and a deception. The "Earth," the more-than-human, like the human itself, eludes us. All manner of unimagined possibilities surround us. How could it be "too late?" Every tomorrow is a new chapter.

Notes

1. Has Environmentalism Forgotten the Earth?

1. Aaron Honori Katcher and Alan M. Beck, "Health and Caring for Living Things," in *Animals and People Sharing the World*, ed. Andrew Rowan (Hanover, N.H.: University Press of New England, 1988), p. 68.

2. Albert Gore, *Earth in the Balance* (Boston: Houghton Mifflin, 1992), pp. 220–21.

3. Ibid., p. 232.

4. Henry David Thoreau, "Walking," in *The Portable Thoreau*, ed. Carl Bode (New York: Viking, 1964), p. 621.

5. Neil Evernden, *The Natural Alien* (Toronto: University of Toronto Press, 1985), pp. 19–20.

6. See Gene Hargrove, "The Gospel of Chief Seattle Is a Hoax," *Environmental Ethics* 11 (1989):195–96.

7. Gary Snyder, *The Old Ways* (San Francisco: City Lights Books, 1977), pp. 35–36.

8. Anne and Paul Ehrlich, *Extinction* (New York: Ballantine, 1981), p. 151.

9. Charles Bergman, *Wild Echoes* (New York: McGraw-Hill, 1990), pp. 51–54.

10. Gore, *Earth in the Balance*, pp. 355–56.

11. Whale researcher Roger Payne, quoted in Diane Ackerman, *The Moon by Whalelight* (New York: Random House, 1991), p. 130.

12. Farley Mowat, *Sea of Slaughter* (Boston: Atlantic Monthly Press, 1984), p. 211.

13. Diane Ackerman, *A Natural History of the Senses* (New York: Vintage, 1991), p. 241; John Hay, "Homing," in *Words from the Land*, ed. Stephen Trimble (Salt Lake City: Peregrine Smith, 1989), pp. 160–61.

14. Lyall Watson, *Gifts of Unknown Things* (Colchester, Vt.: Destiny Books, 1991), p. 27.

15. Thomas Gold, "The Deep, Hot Biosphere," *Proceedings of the*

National Academy of Sciences 89 (1992): 6045–49. For an overview of the developing field, see William Broad, "Strange New Microbes Hint at a Vast Subterranean World," *New York Times*, December 28, 1993, pp. C1, C14.

16. James Lovelock, *Gaia: A New Look at Life on Earth* (New York: Oxford University Press, 1979).

17. Natalie Angier, "Animals and Fungi: Evolutionary Tie?" *Raleigh News and Observer*, April 16, 1993, p. 14A.

18. John Lilly, *Lilly on Dolphins* (Garden City, N.Y.: Anchor Books, 1975), p. 97.

2. Animals Next to Us

1. Sigmund Freud, *Totem and Taboo* (New York: Norton, 1950), pp. 126–27.

2. Konrad Lorenz, *King Solomon's Ring* (New York: Signet, 1972), p. 132.

3. "Dogs Are Really Four-Legged Teens, Researchers Say," *Raleigh News and Observer*, February 16, 1993, p. 3A.

4. John Llewelyn, "Am I Obsessed by Bobby?" in *Re-reading Levinas*, ed. Robert Bernasconi and Simon Critchley (Bloomington: University of Indiana Press, 1991), pp. 234–35.

5. Vicki Hearne, *Adam's Task* (New York: Knopf, 1986), p. 225.

6. Keith Thomas, *Man and the Natural World* (New York: Pantheon, 1983), p. 96.

7. James Serpell, *In the Company of Animals* (Oxford, England: Basil Blackwell, 1986), p. 48; and Kathleen Szasz, *Petishism? Pets and Their People in the Western World* (New York: Holt, Rinehart, and Winston, 1968), p. 13.

8. "Animals in the City," in *New Pespectives on Our Lives with Companion Animals*, ed. A. H. Katcher and A. M. Beck (Philadelphia: University of Pennsylvania Press, 1983), p. 238.

9. Serpell, *In the Company of Animals*, pp. 48–52.

10. Thomas, *Man and the Natural World*, pp. 40, 95.

11. Mary Midgley, *Animals and Why They Matter* (Athens, Ga.: University of Georgia Press, 1983), p. 112.

12. Thomas, *Man and the Natural World*, p. 98.

13. Samuel 12:3.

14. Midgley, *Animals and Why They Matter*, p. 115.

15. Lorenz, *King Solomon's Ring*, p. 173.

16. Ibid., pp. 150–51.

17. Rachel Carson, *The Sea Around Us* (New York: Signet, 1961), p. 93.

18. Charles Darwin, *Voyage of the Beagle* (New York: Penguin, 1989), pp. 48–49, 270, 288–90, 337.

19. Annie Dillard, "Life on the Rocks," in *Words from the Land,* ed. Stephen Trimble (Salt Lake City: Peregrine Smith, 1989), p. 36.

20. Lawrence Slobodkin, *Simplicity and Complexity in Games of the Intellect* (Cambridge: Harvard University Press, 1992), p. 68.

21. Diane Ackerman, *The Moon by Whalelight* (New York: Random House, 1991), pp. 130–31.

22. Iain and Oria Douglas-Hamilton, *Among the Elephants* (New York: Viking, 1975), p. 164.

23. Myron Jacobs, "The Whale Brain," in *Mind in the Waters,* ed. Joan McIntyre (San Francisco: Sierra Club Books, 1974), pp. 82–83.

24. Peter Morgane, "The Whale Brain," in McIntyre, *Mind in the Waters,* pp. 88–89, 92.

25. Carl Sagan, *The Cosmic Connection* (New York: Doubleday, 1973), p. 178.

26. *Encyclopedia of Religion and Philosophy,* 1908. Cited in Midgley, *Animals and Why They Matter*, p. 123.

27. Midgley, *Animals and Why They Matter*, p. 123.

28. Lorenz, *King Solomon's Ring*, p. 96.

29. Ibid., p. 98.

30. Tom Jay, "The Salmon of the Heart," in *Working the Woods, Working the Sea,* ed. Finn Wilcox and Jeremiah Gorsline (Port Townsend, Wash.: Empty Bowl, 1986), p. 116.

31. Paul Shepard, *Animal Thinking* (New York: Viking, 1978).

3. Animals on the Borderlines

1. The description is from Sy Montgomery, *Walking with the Great Apes* (Boston: Houghton Mifflin, 1991), pp. 46–47. I follow Montgomery's accounts throughout this paragraph.

2. Ibid., pp. 102–5.

3. Ibid., pp. 99; and Barbara Noske, *Humans and Other Animals: Beyond the Boundaries of Anthropology* (London: Pluto Press, 1989), p. 152.

4. Montgomery, *Walking with the Great Apes*, pp. 118, 268.

5. Ibid., p. 273.

6. Ibid., p. 31.

7. Ibid., pp. 146–147.

8. Ibid., p. 153.

9. Diane Ackerman, *The Moon by Whalelight* (New York: Random House, 1991), p. 103.

10. Farley Mowat, *Sea of Slaughter* (Boston: Atlantic Monthly Press, 1984), pp. 56, 63–64.

11. Peter Dobra, "Cetaceans: A Litany of Cain," in *People, Penguins, and Plastic Trees*, ed. Donald Vandeveer and Christine Pierce (Belmont, Calif.: Wadsworth, 1986), p. 128.

12. Barry Lopez, *Of Wolves and Men* (New York: Scribner's, 1978), pp. 28–29.

13. Ibid., p. 29.

14. Ibid., p. 52.

15. Mowat, *Sea of Slaughter*, p. 157.

16. L. David Mech, *The Wolf: The Ecology and Behavior of an Endangered Species* (Minneapolis: University of Minnesota Press, 1981), pp. 287–88.

17. Daphne Sheldrick, *The Story of Tsavo* (Indianapolis: Bobbs-Merrill, 1973), p. 107.

18. Jean-Claude Armen, *Gazelle-Boy*, trans. Stephen Hardman (New York: Universe Books, 1974), p. 102. For whales and dolphins, see M. C. Caldwell, D. H. Brown, and D. K. Caldwell, "Intergeneric Behavior by a Captive Pacific Pilot Whale," in *Mind in the Waters*, ed. Joan McIntyre (San Francisco: Sierra Club Books, 1974), pp. 166–67.

19. Diane Ackerman, *A Natural History of the Senses* (New York: Vintage, 1991), p. 266.

20. Noske, *Humans and Other Animals*, p. 162.

21. J.A.L. Singh, "Diary of the Wolf-Children of Midnapore," in J.A.L. Singh and Robert M. Zingg, *Wolf-Children and Feral Man* (Hamden, Conn.: Archon Books, 1966; original, 1833).

22. Bruno Bettelheim, "Feral Children and Autistic Children," *American Journal of Sociology* 64 (1959): 455–67.

23. Lopez, *Of Wolves and Men*, p. 247.

24. Armen, *Gazelle-Boy*, pp. 34–35, 39.

25. Ibid., pp. 98–99.

26. Spinoza, *Ethics*, bk. 3, prop. 2, Scholia.

27. Charles Maclean, *The Wolf Children* (London: Allen Lane, 1977), p. 292.

28. Armen, *Gazelle-Boy*, p. 117.

29. James Serpell, *In the Company of Animals* (Oxford, England: Basil Blackwell, 1986), pp. 50–52. The quotation is from W. E. Roth, "An Introductory Study of the Arts, Crafts, and Customs of the Guiana Indians," *Annual Report of American Ethnology* 38 (1934): 551–56.

30. Serpell, *In the Company of Animals*, p. 35.

31. Charles Doria, "The Dolphin Rider," in McIntyre, *Mind in the Waters*, p. 38.

32. Dobra, "Ceteceans: A Litany of Cain," p. 127.

33. Ackerman, *A Natural History of the Senses*, p. 266.

34. Barry Lopez, *Arctic Dreams* (New York: Bantam, 1986), p. 79.

35. Ibid., p. 96.

36. Ibid., p. 98.

37. Lopez, *Of Wolves and Men*, p. 78.

38. Ibid., p. 85.

39. Mowat, *Sea of Slaughter*, p. 155.

40. Cited in Noske, *Humans and Other Animals*, p. 153. The reference is from Frans B. M. de Wall, ed., *Sociobiologie ter Discussie* (Utrecht and Antwerp: Bohn, Scheltema, en Holkema, 1981), p. 232.

41. Adrian Desmond, *The Ape's Reflection* (New York: Dial Press, 1979), pp. 80–82.

42. Montgomery, *Walking with the Great Apes*, p. 272.

43. Ibid., pp. 150–51, 157.

44. Ibid., p. 264.

45. Henry Beston, *The Outermost House* (New York: Viking, 1961), p. 25.

46. These metaphors are suggested by Montgomery in her last chapter.

47. Diane Ackerman, *The Moon by Whalelight* (New York: Random House, 1991), p. 17.

48. Ibid., pp. 7, 61, 106, 194.

49. Noske, *Humans and Other Animals*, p. 139; Gary Kowalski, *The Souls of Animals* (Walpole, N.H.: Stillpoint Publishing, 1991), chap. 1.

50. Noske, *Humans and Other Animals*, pp. 135–37.

51. Christopher Swan, "The Song That Comes Out of the Sea," *Christian Science Monitor*, March 2, 1987, p. 1.

52. Jane Brody, "Picking Up Mammals' Deep Notes," *New York Times*, November 9, 1993, p. C15.

53. Donald Griffin, *The Question of Animal Awareness* (Los Altos, Calif.: Kaufman, 1981), pp. 41–48, 95, 121.

54. Doris and David Jonas, *Other Senses, Other Worlds* (New York: Stein and Day, 1976), p. 34.

55. Diane Ackerman, "Whale Songs," in *A Natural History of the Senses*, pp. 201–2.

56. Gregory Bateson, *Steps to an Ecology of Mind* (New York: Ballantine, 1972), pp. 364–78.

57. Sterling Bunnell, "The Evolution of Cetacean Intelligence," in McIntyre, *Mind in the Waters*, p. 58.

58. David Abram, "In the Landscape of Language," manuscript, 1992.

59. Mircea Eliade, *Shamanism: Archaic Techniques of Ecstasy*, trans. Willard Trask (Princeton: Princeton University Press, 1964), pp. 96–98.

60. Neil Evernden, *The Natural Alien* (Toronto: University of Toronto Press, 1985), pp. 90–94.

61. Lopez, *Of Wolves and Men*, p. 94.

62. Ibid., p. 62.

63. Evernden, *The Natural Alien*, p. 92.

4. The Land Sings

1. David Abram, "The Perceptual Implications of the Gaia Hypothesis," *The Ecologist* 15 (1988): 98.

2. Diane Ackerman, *A Natural History of the Senses* (New York: Vintage, 1991), pp. 118, 98.

3. T. M. Field, F. Scafidi, and S. Schanberg, "Massage of Preterm Newborns to Improve Growth and Development," *Pediatric Nursing* 13 (1987): 385–87; and Doris and David Jonas, *Other Senses, Other Worlds* (New York: Stein and Day, 1976), p. 145.

4. Ackerman, *A Natural History of the Senses*, p. 118.

5. Jonas and Jonas, *Other Senses, Other Worlds*, p. 19.

6. Ibid., p. 23.

7. Ibid., p. 37.

8. Ackerman, *A Natural History of the Senses*, pp. 122–23.

9. Martha McClintock, "Menstrual Synchrony and Suppression," *Nature* 229 (1971): 244–45.

10. Michael Russell, "Human Olfactory Communication," *Nature* 260 (1976): 520–22.

11. David Howes, "Olfaction and Transition," in *The Varieties of Sensory Experience: A Sourcebook in the Anthropology of the Senses*, ed. David Howes (Toronto: University of Toronto Press, 1991), p. 145.

12. Ivan Illich, *H₂O and the Waters of Forgetfulness* (Dallas: Institute of Humanities and Culture, 1985), pp. 46–67.

13. Ackerman, *A Natural History of the Senses*, p. 39.

14. E. Bruce Goldstein, *Sensation and Perception*, 2nd ed. (Belmont, Calif.: Wadsworth, 1984), p. 407.

15. Philippa Pullar, *Consuming Passions* (Boston: Little, Brown, 1970), p. 37.

16. "Ethnopsychological Aspects of the Terms 'Deaf' and 'Dumb,' " in Howes, *The Varieties of Sensory Experience*, pp. 44–45.

17. Miriam Helen Hill, "Bound to the Environment: Towards a Phenomenology of Sightlessness," in *Dwelling, Place, and Environment*, ed. David Seamon and Robert Mugerauer (Columbia University Press, 1985), p. 105.

18. Helen Keller, *The World I Live In* (New York: Century, 1909), p. 42.

19. Ackerman, *A Natural History of the Senses*, p. xviii.

20. Hill, "Bound to the Environment," p. 108.

21. Lyall Watson, *Gifts of Unknown Things* (Colchester, Vt.: Destiny Books, 1991), p. 116.

22. Hill, "Bound to the Environment," p. 105.

23. Tom Sullivan and Derek Gill, *If You Could See What I Hear* (New York: Harper and Row, 1975), pp. 10, 68.

24. Jonas and Jonas, *Other Senses, Other Worlds*, p. 30.

25. Maurice Merleau-Ponty, *Phenomenology of Perception*, trans. Colin Smith (New York: Humanities Press, 1962), pp. 229–30.

26. Tony Hiss, *The Experience of Place* (New York: Vintage, 1990), p. 20.

27. Merleau-Ponty, *Phenomenology of Perception*, p. 29.

28. Constance Classen, "The Sensory Orders of 'Wild Children,' " in Howes, *The Varieties of Sensory Experience*, p. 50.

29. Ibid., pp. 50–54.

30. Ibid., p. 59.

31. Anselm von Feuerbach, "Caspar Hauser," in *Wolf-Children and Feral Man*, ed. J.A.L. Singh and R. M. Zingg (Hamden, Conn.: Archon Books, 1966; original, 1833), p. 356.

32. Sy Montgomery, *Walking with the Great Apes* (Boston: Houghton Mifflin, 1991), p. 179.

33. Barry Lopez, *Of Wolves and Men* (New York: Scribner's 1978), p. 82.

34. Bill Mollison, *Permaculture: A Practical Guide for a Sustainable Future* (Washington, D.C.: Island Press, 1990), pp. 97–98.

35. A. R. Radcliffe-Brown, *The Andaman Islanders* (New York: Free Press, 1964), pp. 311–12.

36. Walter Ong, "The Shifting Sensorium," in Howes, *The Varieties of Sensory Experience.*

37. Lopez, *Of Wolves and Men,* pp. 247–48.

38. Calvin Martin, *In the Spirit of the Earth* (Baltimore: Johns Hopkins University Press, 1992), p. 7.

39. Roderick Nash, "Preface to the Third Edition," *Wilderness and the American Mind* (New Haven: Yale University Press, 1982), p. xiv.

40. Luther Standing Bear, *Land of the Spotted Eagle* (Lincoln: University of Nebraska Press, 1978), p. 38.

41. Gary Snyder, *The Practice of the Wild* (San Francisco: North Point Press, 1990), p. 7.

42. Nash, *Wilderness and the American Mind,* p. 277. Interview with William Brown, National Park Service, Anchorage, Alaska, August 26, 1980.

43. Ackerman, *A Natural History of the Senses,* p. 12.

44. Ibid., p. 13.

45. Walt Whitman, "Out of the Cradle Endlessly Rocking," in *Leaves of Grass* (New York: Norton, 1973), p. 246.

46. Gary Snyder, *The Old Ways: Six Essays* (San Francisco: City Lights Books, 1977), pp. 35–36.

47. Richard Nelson, *Make Prayers to the Raven* (Chicago: University of Chicago Press, 1983), p. 115.

48. Keith Thomas, *Man and the Natural World* (New York: Pantheon, 1983), pp. 96, 98.

49. Ackerman, *A Natural History of the Senses,* p. 215.

50. Bruce Chatwin, *The Songlines* (London: Penguin, 1989), p. 108.

51. Mollison, *Permaculture,* pp. 96–97.

52. Colin Fletcher, *The Complete Walker* (New York: Knopf, 1970), p. 7.

53. Jack Turner, "The Abstract Wild," *Witness* 3, no. 4 (Winter 1989): 88.

54. Thomas Lyons, "The Saving Wilderness," *Wild Earth*, Summer 1992, p. 3.

55. Lyall Watson, *Heaven's Breath: A Natural History of the Wind* (London: Hodder and Stoughton, 1984), p. 30.

56. David Rains Wallace, *The Klamath Knot* (San Francisco: Sierra Club Books, 1983), p. 19.

57. Henry David Thoreau, "Ktaadn," in *The Maine Woods* (Princeton: Princeton University Press, 1972), p. 61.

58. Lyall Watson, *Gifts of Unknown Things*, p. 87.

59. Henry David Thoreau, "Walden," in *The Portable Thoreau*, ed. Carl Bode (New York: Viking, 1964), p. 542.

60. Ackerman, *A Natural History of the Senses*, pp. 222–23.

61. Ibid., p. 309.

62. James Lovelock, *Gaia: A New Theory of Life on Earth* (New York: Oxford University Press, 1979).

63. Richard Kerr, "No Longer Willful, Gaia Becomes Respectable," *Science* 240 (April 22, 1988): 393–95.

64. Ackerman, *A Natural History of the Senses*, pp. 236–37.

5. Desolation

1. Roderick Nash, *Wilderness and the American Mind*, 3rd ed. (New Haven: Yale University Press, 1982), p. xvi.

2. For these stories and many more, see Farley Mowat, *Sea of Slaughter* (Boston: Atlantic Monthly Press, 1984).

3. Paul and Anne Ehrlich, *Extinction* (New York: Ballantine, 1981), p. 137.

4. Mowat, *Sea of Slaughter*, pp. 135, 139, 141.

5. Ibid., pp. 294–95.

6. Ibid., p. 218.

7. "Settlement Breaks Species-Protection Gridlock," *Washington Post* wire story, *Raleigh News and Observer*, December 16, 1992, p. A3.

8. William Stevens, "Botanists Contrive Comebacks for Threatened Plants," *New York Times*, May 11, 1993, pp. C1.

9. Peter Dobra, "Cetaceans: A Litany of Cain," in *People, Penguins, and Plastic Trees*, ed. Donald Vandeveer and Christine Pierce (Belmont, Calif.: Wadsworth, 1986), p. 130.

10. Mowat, *Sea of Slaughter*, pp. 263–64.

11. Diana McMeekin, "Mrithi: 1968–1992," *Christian Science Monitor*, June 15, 1992, p. 19.

12. Ehrlich and Ehrlich, *Extinction*, p. 6.

13. "Astronauts Will Dump Faulty Panel," *Raleigh News and Observer*, December 6, 1993, p. 7A.

14. Barry Lopez, *Of Wolves and Men* (New York: Scribner's, 1978), pp. 14–16.

15. Diane Ackerman, *The Moon by Whalelight* (New York: Random House, 1991), p. 46–47.

16. Dobra, "Cetaceans: A Litany of Cain," pp. 127, 130–31.

17. Victor Scheffer, "The Case for a World Moratorium on Whaling," in *Mind in the Waters*, ed. Joan McIntyre (San Francisco: Sierra Club Books, 1974), p. 229.

18. Albert Gore, *Earth in the Balance* (Boston: Houghton Mifflin, 1992), p. 119.

19. Susanna Hecht and Alexander Cockburn, *The Fate of the Forest* (New York: Verso, 1989).

20. Mowat, *Sea of Slaughter*, pp. 139–40.

21. Tom Jay, "The Salmon of the Heart," in *Working the Woods, Working the Sea*, ed. Finn Wilcox and Jeremiah Gorsline (Port Townsend, Wash.: Empty Bowl, 1986), p. 111n.

22. Peter Steinhart, "Quiet, Please," *Audubon*, May 1984, p. 10.

23. Malcolm Browne, "Human Noises in Ocean Held to Threaten Marine Mammals," *New York Times*, October 19, 1993, pp. C1, C12.

24. Barry Lopez, *Arctic Dreams* (New York: Bantam, 1986), p. 125.

25. Greg Kilbane, "Starlight Memories," *In These Times*, August 7–20, 1991, p. 24.

26. Ibid.

27. Chet Raymo, *The Virgin and the Mousetrap: Essays in Search of the Soul of Science* (New York: Viking, 1991), pp. 14–15.

28. William Strauss, "If It's East of the Mississippi, It's Blanketed in Pollution's Haze," *New York Times*, July 16, 1990, p. C4.

29. Gary Snyder, *The Practice of the Wild* (San Francisco: North Point Press, 1990), p. 82.

30. Michael Pollan, *Second Nature* (New York: Atlantic Monthly Press, 1991), p. 230.

31. Mowat, *Sea of Slaughter*, p. 404.

32. Nash, *Wilderness and the American Mind*, p. 192.

33. Peter Singer, *Animal Liberation*, 2nd ed. (New York: Avon, 1991), chap. 3.

34. James Serpell, *In the Company of Animals* (Oxford: Basil Blackwell, 1986), pp. 9–10.

35. D. Wise and A. Jennings, "Dyschondroplasia in Domestic Poultry," *Veterinary Record* 91 (1972): 285–86. Cited in Singer, *Animal Liberation*, p. 104.

36. Bill McKibben, *The End of Nature* (New York: Random House, 1989), p. 165.

37. Frederick Douglass, "The Claims of the Negro Ethnologically Considered," in *The Frederick Douglass Papers* (New Haven: Yale University Press, 1982), series 1, vol. 2 p. 507.

38. Bruno Bettleheim, *The Informed Heart* (New York: Free Press, 1960).

39. Jim Nollman, *Dolphin Dreamtime* (New York: Bantam, 1987), pp. 94–97.

40. Singer, *Animal Liberation*, pp. 67–68.

41. Mary Midgley, *Beast and Man* (Ithaca, N.Y.: Cornell University Press, 1978), p. 229–30.

42. Singer, *Animal Liberation*, pp. 99, 104.

43. Mowat, *Sea of Slaughter*, pp. 97–98.

44. Charles Bergmann, *Wild Echoes* (New York: McGraw-Hill, 1990), p. 119.

45. Ackerman, *The Moon by Whalelight*, p. 117.

46. Lopez, *Of Wolves and Men*, p. 81.

47. Exodus 34:13–14.

48. Serpell, *In the Company of Animals*, p. 75.

49. Hans Peter Duerr, *Dreamtime: Concerning the Boundary between Wilderness and Civilization* (Oxford: Basil Blackwell, 1985), p. 30.

50. Jean Baudrillard, *Simulations* (New York: Semiotext[e], 1983).

51. Alston Chase, *Playing God in Yellowstone: The Destruction of America's First National Park* (New York: Harcourt Brace Jovanovich, 1986), pp. 201–3.

52. Jack Turner, "The Abstract Wild," *Witness* 3, no. 4 (Winter 1989): 89.

53. Albert Borgmann, *Technology and the Character of Contemporary Life* (Chicago: University of Chicago Press, 1984), p. 56.

54. Turner, "The Abstract Wild," p. 89.

55. Nash, *Wilderness and the American Mind.* pp. 225–26.

56. Ackerman, *The Moon by Whalelight,* p. 86.

57. Lance Morrow, "Trashing Mount Sinai," *Time,* March 19, 1990, p. 92.

58. Ibid.

59. Job 38:6–9.

60. Peter Steinhart, quoted by Gary Nabhan in "Representing the Lives of Plants and Animals," *Wild Earth,* Spring 1992, p. 3. Nabhan does not give a citation.

61. Thomas Lyons, "The Saving Wilderness," *Wild Earth,* Summer 92, p. 3.

62. Bergman, *Wild Echoes,* p. 104.

6. Coming to Our Senses

1. The Ecostery Foundation of North America: Statement of Philosophy," *The Trumpeter* 7, no. 1 (1990): 12–16.

2. Henry David Thoreau, "Ktaadn," in *The Maine Woods* (Princeton: Princeton University Press, 1972), p. 71.

3. Christopher Alexander et al., *A Pattern Language* (New York: Oxford University Press, 1977), p. 303.

4. Ibid., pp. 136–37, 307–8, 372–73, 509–11, 518–19, 544–47.

5. Wendell Berry, "Getting Along with Nature," in *Home Economics* (San Francisco: North Point Press, 1987), p. 13.

6. Alexander, *A Pattern Language,* p. 360.

7. Ibid., pp. 514–16, 562–63, 614–17, 747–51.

8. Ibid., p. 787.

9. Ibid., pp. 752–68.

10. M. L. von Franz, "The Process of Individuation," in C. G. Jung, *Man and His Symbols* (New York: Doubleday, 1964), pp. 161–64.

11. Alexander, *A Pattern Language,* pp. 794–817. On "edible landscape" as an Alexanderian pattern, see "Promoting a Foundational Ecology Practically through Christopher Alexander's Pattern Language," in David Seamon, ed., *Dwelling, Seeing, and Designing* (Albany, N.Y.: SUNY Press, 1993), p. 337.

12. J. Donald Hughes and Jim Swan, "How Much of the Earth Is Sacred Space?" *Environmental Review* 10 (1986): 248; and Vincent Scully, *The Earth, The Temple, and the Gods* (New Haven: Yale University Press, 1979).

13. Lyall Watson, *Gifts of Unknown Things* (Colchester, Vt.: Destiny Books, 1991), p. 115.

14. Ibid., p. 113.

15. I draw in part on Daniel Dustin, "Gardening as a Subversive Activity," address to the Northeastern Recreation Research Symposium, Saratoga Springs, N.Y., April 7, 1991.

16. Michael Pollan, *Second Nature* (New York: Atlantic Monthly Press, 1991), p. 111.

17. Ibid., 109.

18. Sara B. Stein, *My Weeds.* Quoted in ibid., p. 110. Pollan does not give a citation.

19. Euell Gibbons, *Stalking the Wild Asparagus* (New York: McKay, 1962).

20. *Seeds Blum* ($3 from Seeds Blum, Idaho City Stage, Boise, Idaho 83706) is a seed catalog for "heirloom" seeds interspersed with an extended discussion of the politics of the seed industry.

21. Pollan, *Second Nature,* pp. 190–96.

22. Tony Hiss, *The Experience of Place* (New York: Vintage, 1990), pp. 114–15.

23. Wendell Berry, "Getting Along with Nature," in *Home Economics* (San Francisco: North Point Press, 1987), p. 13.

24. Dave Foreman, "Putting the Earth First," *Confessions of an Eco-Warrior* (New York: Harmony Books, 1991), pp. 25–36; Murray Bookchin, "Which Way for the US Greens?" *New Politics* 11, no. 2 (Winter 1989); and Bill Devall, "Deep Ecology and Its Critics," *Earth First!* December 22, 1987.

25. Hans Peter Duerr, *Dreamtime: Concerning the Boundary between Wilderness and Civilization* (Oxford: Basil Blackwell, 1985).

26. Gary Snyder, *The Practice of the Wild* (San Francisco: North Point Press, 1990), p. 93.

27. Ibid., p. 14.

28. Bill McKibben, "A Proposal for a Park without Fences," *Wild Earth,* Spring 1993, p. 65.

29. Ward Churchill, *Struggle for the Land* (Monroe, Me.: Common Courage Press, 1993), pp. 423–31.

30. Sara Stein, *Noah's Garden* (Boston: Houghton Mifflin, 1993), p. 140.

31. Ibid., pp. 47–51.

32. John Elder, *Imagining the Earth* (Chicago: University of Illinois Press, 1985), p. 80.

33. A. R. Ammons, "Corsons Inlet," in *Corson's Inlet* (Ithaca, N.Y.: Cornell University Press, 1965), p. 5.

34. Pollan, *Second Nature*, p. 63.

35. Wendell Berry, *What Are People For?* (San Francisco: North Point Press, 1990), p. 200.

36. Helen and Newt Harrison, public address at the School of Design, North Carolina State University, November 1992.

37. Hiss, *The Experience of Place*, p. 147.

38. Ibid., pp. 162–67.

39. Ibid., pp. 189–95.

40. Alexander, *A Pattern Language*, pp. 270–75, 280–92.

41. Arthur Waskow, *Seasons of Our Joy* (Boston: Beacon Press, 1982), p. 92.

42. Antler, "Star-Struck Utopias of 2000," *The Trumpeter* 9 (1992): 180.

43. Charlene Spretnak, "Ecofeminism: Our Roots and Flowering," in *Reweaving the World: The Emergence of Ecofeminism*, ed. Irene Diamond et al. (San Francisco: Sierra Club Books, 1990), p. 13.

7. Transhuman Etiquettes

1. Vicki Hearne, *Adam's Task* (New York: Knopf, 1986), pp. 229–30.

2. Carol Adams, "Abortion Rights and Animal Rights," *Between the Species*, Fall 1991, p. 185.

3. Sy Montgomery, *Walking with the Great Apes* (Boston: Houghton Mifflin, 1991), p. 30.

4. Doris and David Jonas, *Other Senses, Other Worlds* (New York: Stein and Day, 1976), p. 109.

5. Keith Thomas, *Man and the Natural World* (New York: Pantheon, 1983), pp. 96–97, 113–14.

6. Carol Cina, "Regenderizing Other Animals as 'She,' " *The Trumpeter* 9 (1992): 156.

7. Calvin Martin, *In the Spirit of the Earth* (Baltimore: Johns Hopkins University Press, 1992), p. 29.

8. Ibid., p. 103.

9. Gary Kowalski, *The Souls of Animals* (Walpole, N.H.: Stillpoint Publishing, 1991), p. 87.

10. D. H. Lawrence, "A Doe at Eveing," in *The Complete Poems of D. H. Lawrence,* ed. Vivian de Sola Pinto and Warren Roberts (New York: Viking, 1964), 1:122.

11. Jane Goodall, *In the Shadow of Man* (Boston: Houghton Mifflin, 1971), p. 271.

12. Mary Midgley, *Animals and Why They Matter* (Athens, Ga.: University of Georgia Press, 1983), p. 113.

13. Tom Regan, *The Case for Animal Rights* (Berkeley: University of California Press, 1983); and Peter Singer, *Animal Liberation,* 2nd ed. (New York: Avon Books, 1992).

14. Regan, *The Case for Animal Rights,* pp. 218–28.

15. Singer, *Animal Liberation,* pp. i–ii.

16. Ibid., p. ii.

17. Mary Midgley, *Beast and Man* (Ithaca, N.Y.: Cornell University Press, 1978), pp. 229–30.

18. Sy Montgomery, *Walking with the Great Apes* (Boston: Houghton Mifflin, 1991), p. 265–66.

19. Eugene Linden, *Silent Partners: The Legacy of the Ape Language Experiments* (New York: Ballantine, 1986).

20. Michael J. Roads, *Talking with Nature* (Tiburon, Calif.: H. J. Kramer, 1985).

21. Barry Lopez, *Of Wolves and Men* (New York: Scribner's, 1978), p. 80.

22. Jim Nollman, "What Seagull Says to the Orca," in *Dolphin Dreamtime* (New York: Bantam, 1987).

23. Sterling Bunnell, "The Evolution of Cetacean Intelligence," in *Mind in the Waters,* ed. Joan McIntyre (San Francisco: Sierra Club Books, 1974), p. 56.

24. Paul Spong, "The Whale Show," in McIntyre, *Mind in the Waters,* p. 176.

25. Ibid., pp. 176–84.

26. Nollman, *Dolphin Dreamtime,* pp. 146–50.

27. Ibid., p. 148.

28. Ibid., pp. 158–59.

29. Ibid., pp. 159–60.

30. Ibid., p. 164.

31. Gary Kowalski, *The Souls of Animals*, p. 34.

32. Kenneth Brower, "The Naked Vulture and the Thinking Ape," *Atlantic Monthly*, October 1983, pp. 70–88.

33. Diane Ackerman, *The Moon by Whalelight* (New York: Random House, 1991), pp. 64–65.

34. Ibid., p. 64.

35. Kowalski, *The Souls of Animals*, pp. 41–49; David Gucwa and James Ehmann, *To Whom It May Concern* (New York: Norton, 1985); and Jane Goodall, *The Chimps of Gombe* (Cambridge: Harvard University Press, 1986), pp. 26, 41.

36. Gerald Hausman, *Meditations with Animals* (Santa Fe: Bear and Company, 1986), p. 34.

8. Is It Too Late?

1. Malcolm Browne, "City Lights and Space Ads May Blind Stargazers," *New York Times*, May 4, 1993, p. C1.

2. Cecil Eby, *"That Disgraceful Affair": The Black Hawk War* (New York: Norton, 1973).

3. Amory Lovins, *Soft Energy Paths* (New York: Harper and Row, 1977).

4. John Kling, "Urban Creeks Going Natural," *San Francisco Chronicle*, October 26, 1993, p. A1. George Sessions pointed out this article to me.

5. Heidi Fischer, "Ecological by Design," *Utne Reader*, July/August 1993, p. 46.

6. Kirkpatrick Sale, "The US Green Movement Today," *The Nation*, July 19, 1993, p. 92.

7. Sanjoy Hazarika, "Sect in India Guards Desert Wildlife," *New York Times*, February 2, 1993, p. C4.

8. On the points made in this paragraph, see Christopher Stone, *The Gnat Is Older Than Man* (Princeton: Princeton University Press, 1993), pp. 20–23.

9. Steven Schneider, "The Changing Climate," *Scientific American* 261 (September 1989): 73.

10. Michael Lemonick, "Rewriting the Book on Dinosaurs," *Time*, April 26, 1993, p. 43.

11. R. A. Kerr, "Fugitive Carbon Dioxide: It's Not Hiding in the Ocean," *Science* 256 (1992): 35.

12. Keith Thomson, *Living Fossil: The Story of the Coelacanth* (New York: Norton, 1991).

13. Malcolm Browne, "Two Clues Back Idea That Birds Arose from Dinosaurs," *New York Times,* December 28, 1993, pp. C1, C9.

Index